The Michigan
DIVORCE BOOK
A guide to doing an uncontested divorce without an attorney
without minor children

By Michael Maran • Michigan Attorney

Grand River Press
P.O. Box 1342
E. Lansing, MI 48826

The Michigan Divorce Book: A Guide to Doing an Uncontested Divorce without an Attorney (without minor children)
by Michael Maran

Published by:
Grand River Press
P.O. Box 1342
E. Lansing, MI 48826

Printing history:
First edition: January 1986
Second edition:
  First printing: June 1989
  Second printing: September 1990
Third edition:
  First printing: May 1993
  Second printing: October 1994
  Third printing: January 1996
Fourth edition: February 1998

ISBN 0-936343-10-9
Printed in the United States of America

Order Form

■ **The Michigan Divorce Book: A Guide to Doing an Uncontested Divorce without an Attorney (without minor children)** $24.95

    Update $1.00

■ **The Michigan Divorce Book: A Guide to Doing an Uncontested Divorce without an Attorney (with minor children)** $29.95

    Update $1.50

TITLE	PRICE	QUANTITY	TOTAL

Subtotal	
Add 6% Sales Tax	
Postage	$2.50
TOTAL	

Method of Payment:

☐ Check or money order (payable to **Grand River Press**)
☐ Charge: ☐ Visa ☐ MasterCard

Account # ☐☐☐☐☐☐☐☐☐☐☐☐☐☐☐☐☐☐☐☐

_____

Expiration Date   Signature

_____

Name

_____

Address

_____

City   State   Zip

Please send form to: **Grand River Press, P.O. Box 1342, East Lansing, Michigan 48826**

Dedication:
V. Cramer

Illustrations:
Patric Fourshe

Lettering and layout:
Altese Graphic Design

Editing:
Mark Woodbury

Contents

Chapter 2

Doing Your Divorce

Appendices

Forms

Preface

Do your own divorce? The idea may sound crazy to many people. After all, doesn't everyone need a lawyer to get a divorce?

The fact is, you have the right to do your own divorce, just as you have the right to represent yourself in any legal matter. The right of legal self-representation is so important it's protected by the Bill of Rights in the U.S. Constitution (it falls under the First Amendment's right of petition for redress of grievances). In Michigan, legal self-help is also guaranteed by Sec. 13 of Art. 1 of the Michigan Constitution of 1963, which says: "a suitor in any court of this state has the right to prosecute or defend his suit, either *in his own proper person* or by an attorney." (Emphasis added.)

Despite these guarantees, the right to represent yourself in court doesn't mean very much if you don't know what you're doing once you get there. That's where this book comes in.

Chapter 1 describes divorce, tells you what an uncontested divorce is and helps you decide whether you can handle it yourself. Chapter 2 has instructions and sample forms to guide you through a divorce. And last but not least, blank forms are included in the back of the book which you can tear out and use to file your own divorce case.

Chapter 1

PART I: Introduction to Divorce

PART II: Uncontested Divorce

PART III: Doing an Uncontested Divorce Yourself

PART I:
Introduction to Divorce

Asked about the origin of divorce, the French philosopher Voltaire said he didn't know exactly, but assumed that divorce was invented a few weeks after marriage. His reasoning? A couple married, quarreled, and were ready for divorce a few weeks later.

Although it was meant as a joke, Voltaire's remark wasn't that far from the truth. Divorce *has* been around almost as long as marriage. The Babylonian Code of Hammurabi, the oldest known code of law, authorized divorce on several grounds, including a wife's barrenness, disloyalty, neglect or disease. According to the Bible, a Hebrew husband could divorce his wife for "uncleanness" by giving her a "bill of divorcement" and sending her packing.

It was this law that Jesus was quizzed about by the Pharisees when they asked him: "Is it lawful for a man to divorce his wife?" The Gospel of St. Mark says Jesus condemned the practice, adding: "What therefore God hath joined together, let not man put asunder." Yet St. Matthew's account of this incident is contradictory. It says that Jesus permitted divorce on grounds of wives' "fornication." Other New Testament scripture is also inconsistent; some passages are hostile to divorce, while others seem to tolerate it.

With all this confusion, the Bible can be interpreted to either allow or disallow divorce. Catholic countries sided with the Mark Gospel and placed a strict ban on divorce. But Protestant countries—with the notable exception of England—followed Matthew and allowed divorce on grounds of adultery and sometimes desertion.

When it came to law, America usually took its cue from England, so it should have observed the English ban on divorce. But divorce became firmly established in this country after the first American divorce was granted in

1639 by the Massachusetts Bay Colony to Mrs. James Luxford for her husband's bigamy.

There were several reasons for that. In a way, America itself was the child of divorce: the "divorce," in the guise of the American Revolution, from England. It's even possible to read the Declaration of Independence as the petition for that divorce. This interpretation isn't as far-fetched as it seems.

Thomas Jefferson, the author of the Declaration of Independence, had handled divorce cases as a young lawyer, and the catalog of grievances and wrongs found in the declaration echoed those from his divorce practice.

There were also practical reasons for the American love affair with divorce. During the colonial era, divorce was forbidden in England, France, Italy and several other European countries. Many immigrants to America were fleeing these repressive divorce laws as much as religious or political persecution. Once here, they were in no mood for tough European-style divorce laws.

By the mid-19th century, almost all the states had divorce laws. Typically, these laws permitted divorce on a variety of fault grounds. According to this fault system, divorce was available only when one spouse had committed marital misconduct. This gave the faultless spouse grounds for a divorce.

On the other hand, an at-fault spouse wasn't entitled to get a divorce. A peculiar divorce doctrine called recrimination prevented anyone with "unclean hands" from asking for a divorce. Recrimination effectively barred an at-fault spouse (who was often the one who wanted out of the marriage the most) from getting a divorce, unless the faultless spouse was willing to excuse the marital misconduct. By using this divorce veto, the faultless spouse could blackmail the at-fault spouse—by demanding extra property, support or other concessions—as the price for the divorce.

During this era, Michigan divorce law was typical of the fault divorce laws. The 1846 divorce law had seven fault grounds for divorce: 1) adultery 2) physical incompetence 3) imprisonment 4) desertion 5) husband's drunkenness 6) extreme cruelty 7) husband's neglect. It also had a firm policy against recrimination.

But not every state was as generous with divorce grounds as Michigan. Before 1967, New York had a notoriously strict divorce law, which allowed divorce only on grounds of adultery. South Carolina was even worse. Divorce was legalized in that state after the Civil War and then abolished in 1878. Divorce was finally re-established in South Carolina in 1949, after an absence of 71 years!

When people were frustrated by strict divorce laws in their home states, they often fled to other states with better laws. This so-called migratory divorce was possible because the United States, unlike most countries, doesn't have a uniform national divorce law. Instead, divorce is regulated by each state. With 50 different divorce laws, it's no wonder that migratory divorce has been a problem in America since colonial times.

Many states tried to stop migratory divorce by adopting divorce residency requirements or erecting other barriers. But a handful of states encouraged divorce migration as a boost to local tourism. One state—Nevada—even managed to make migratory divorce its largest industry. In 1907, William Schnitzer, a sharp New York lawyer, noticed that Nevada had a lax divorce law, with a short residency period, seven grounds for divorce and no recrimination doctrine. Schnitzer opened an office in Reno and soon divorce migrants flocked there. Other lawyers followed in Schnitzer's footsteps and migratory divorce flourished in Nevada.

As easy as migratory divorce was, it was still very expensive. There was the cost of getting the divorce, not to mention the expense of traveling to another state and living there during the residency period. As a result, migratory divorce was a luxury only the wealthy could afford.

Among those making the trek to Nevada was Nelson Rockefeller, then governor of New York. Millionaire Rockefeller got a Nevada divorce in 1962 while thousands of his fellow New Yorkers were trapped at home without a divorce remedy. Rockefeller's divorce caused a furor, and many think it cost him the Republican presidential nomination in 1964.

By the 1960s, all the controversy over migratory divorce had created a mood for change. California took the first step in 1969 when it adopted a "no-fault" divorce law. Previously, California had a fault divorce law with several fault grounds (adultery, extreme cruelty, willful neglect, etc.). It replaced these with two no-fault grounds: incurable insanity and irreconcilable differences. What's more, the new California law banished fault from the other divorce issues of alimony, child support and property division.

The California no-fault law revolutionized divorce in America, as other states rushed to enact similar no-fault laws. Within five years, 45 states had adopted no-fault divorce. By 1986, when final holdout South Dakota gave in, every state had some type of no-fault divorce.

Michigan was among the first states to adopt no-fault divorce in the early 1970s. But in Michigan the transition from fault to no-fault divorce wasn't as smooth as it was in other states. At first, Michigan lawmakers were poised to adopt a sweeping California-style no-fault divorce law removing fault from divorce entirely. Michigan lawyers were horrified at this idea because they feared that no-fault divorce meant no-lawyer divorce. The lawyers lobbied furiously against the no-fault proposal. Ultimately, a deal was reached providing for no-fault divorce grounds, but with fault left intact for most of the other divorce issues. This no-fault divorce law took effect on January. 1, 1972, and is still the law today.

In the last few years, no-fault divorce has stirred up new controversy. Feminists have complained that no-fault divorce can be unfair to women. Their reasoning: no-fault destroyed the divorce leverage women once had, leading to smaller property division and support settlements for them. Some conservatives argue that no-fault divorce actually encourages divorce, bringing more of the social problems associated with divorce.

In Michigan, no-fault critics have introduced bills in the legislature to repeal parts of the no-fault law, and reintroduce fault into divorce grounds. These proposals got a lot of press, but haven't gone anywhere as legislators have shied away from re-opening the debate on no-fault divorce.

Do-It-Yourself Divorce

During the era of fault divorce, few dared to do their own divorces because they were hard to handle. But a no-fault divorce is really just a clerical task, which even a nonlawyer can manage. As soon as no-fault laws were adopted, nonlawyer entrepreneurs set up do-it-yourself divorce services to help people do their own divorces.

In Michigan, two such operations sprang up in 1972 after the no-fault divorce law went into effect: Harry Gordon Associates in Oak Park and Gordon, Graham and Cramer in Detroit. Harry Gordon Associates sold a divorce kit with forms and instructions. Gordon, Graham and Cramer offered personalized services, including preparation of papers, filing and help with court appearances.

Alarmed at this threat to their business, Michigan lawyers sought to enforce the unauthorized practice of law statute against their new rivals. Like most states, Michigan has an unauthorized practice law barring non-lawyers from practicing law. This law permits you to represent yourself, but you must be a lawyer to represent others.

In 1972, courts invoked this law and ordered Harry Gordon Associates and Gordon, Graham and Cramer out of business. Facing jail if they disobeyed, most of the firms' operators reluctantly closed. But Virginia Cramer, one of the partners in Gordon, Graham and Cramer, refused to be intimidated. She re-emerged with a new divorce service similar to her old one. Just like before, lawyers tried to stop her claiming that she was engaged in the unauthorized practice of law.

After battling in court for several years, the parties ended up before the Michigan Supreme Court in the case known as *State Bar of Michigan v. Cramer*. The issue in the case was whether Cramer had violated the unauthorized practice law by providing personalized legal services. The court decided that she had when she gave clients *specific* legal information (telling them what to do in their particular situations). On the other hand, the court said that nonlawyers like Cramer could offer *general* legal information in the form of books or legal kits.

Thanks to the apparent ban on nonlawyer divorce services, few such firms exist in Michigan. Without this option, most divorce do-it-yourselfers have had to rely on self-help divorce books or kits. Since the 1970s, several legal aid organizations and women's groups have offered do-it-yourself divorce kits. This book has its genesis in one such kit published in 1981. It was enlarged into book form in 1986, and revised several times since then.

PART II: Uncontested Divorce

Before you start your divorce, it's important to talk with your spouse and see if you agree on the divorce issues. This will determine whether your divorce will be contested or uncontested.

A disagreement over the divorce issues usually means a contested divorce. You are entitled to represent yourself in a contested divorce. But your spouse would probably get a lawyer, giving him/her an edge over you during the divorce. That's why you shouldn't represent yourself in a contested case.

On the other hand, if you and your spouse agree on all the divorce issues, you have an uncontested divorce. You ought to be able to handle this kind of divorce yourself without a lawyer. But see Part III for several situations in which even an uncontested divorce may be too complicated for you to do yourself.

What sort of agreement do you need for an uncontested divorce? A formal written agreement—called a separation or settlement agreement—won't be necessary. Michigan doesn't require these in uncontested cases, as some states do. Instead, an informal agreement or understanding should be enough.

Sometimes you may not need an agreement at all. Needless to say, it's impossible to discuss divorce with a spouse who has disappeared. In that case, the spouse's absence should permit you to go ahead and get an uncontested divorce just as if s/he were agreeing to it.

Divorce Issues

During your talk, you and your spouse may quickly agree that your marriage must end. But a divorce is more than simply ending a marriage. In a divorce with minor children, there are a lot of divorce issues dealing with the children. Even in divorces without minor children, there are three important divorce issues:

- end of marriage
- property division
- alimony

These are the issues you and your spouse must agree on to have an uncontested divorce. To help you reach agreement, the rest of this chapter examines these issues in detail.

End of Marriage

Above all else, a divorce means ending your marriage. To accomplish that, you need specific grounds (reasons). As explained in Part I, Michigan once had fault grounds, such as adultery, desertion, extreme cruelty, etc., for divorce. But in 1972, Michigan adopted the following no-fault grounds for divorce:

There has been a breakdown of the marriage relationship to the extent that the objects of matrimony have been destroyed and there remains no reasonable likelihood that the marriage can be preserved.

If you look at these grounds closely, you can see that three things must exist to get a divorce: 1) a marital breakdown ("breakdown of the marriage relationship") 2) that is serious ("to the extent that the objects of matrimony have been destroyed") 3) and permanent ("there remains no reasonable likelihood that the marriage can be preserved").

At first, when the no-fault law was new, courts had trouble applying the no-fault grounds. Judges continued to probe into the reasons for marital breakdowns, as they had under the old fault law. Some judges even denied divorces when they felt that a marriage hadn't really broken down or could be saved.

But by the late 1970s, courts were applying the no-fault law more liberally. These days, courts don't investigate the marital breakdown very much, and divorces are granted for almost any reason. As a result, the end of the marriage issue is seldom contested in divorces any more.

Glossary

Uncontested divorce–divorce where spouses agree on all the divorce issues.

No-fault divorce–all Michigan divorces, whether contested or uncontested, are no-fault divorces since they must use no-fault grounds.

Property Division

Years ago, divorce property division was little more than divvying up pots, pans, clothing and personal effects. But today a lot more may be at stake. *Forbes* magazine recently listed the women receiving the largest divorce property divisions. Topping the list were Anne Bass, ex-wife of real estate magnate Sid Bass ($200 million), Frances Lear, who divorced Norman Lear, producer of *All in the Family* and *Maude*, ($112 million), and actress Amy Irving, ex-wife of filmmaker Steven Spielberg ($100 million).

What all these divorces have in common is that they happened in either Texas or California, which are community property states. In these states, marriage is considered an equal financial partnership, so most property acquired during a marriage belongs to the spouses equally, regardless of which spouse earned or owned it. And when a marriage ends—by death or divorce—each spouse gets one-half of the marital property.

Only nine states, mostly in the South and West, have community property. The rest, including Michigan, have a different system of property ownership and division. At one time, Michigan divided property during divorce strictly according to ownership: Each spouse got whatever they owned. This system was simple and neat, but it discriminated against wives because husbands usually owned most property.

Accused of unfairness, Michigan adopted an equitable distribution system of property division in divorce cases. Like community property law, equitable distribution recognizes that marriage is a financial partnership, giving each spouse a share of the property regardless of ownership.

Despite that similarity, community property and equitable distribution divide property very differently. Spouses always get equal shares of community property. In equitable distribution, the shares can be equal or unequal. All the law asks is that the division be "just and reasonable" or "equitable" under the circumstances.

The flexibility of equitable distribution shows up in court decisions. For example, in Michigan divorces wives have gotten as much as 90% or as little as 10% of the property. Under equitable distribution, such lopsided divisions are permissible if justified by the facts of the case. Nevertheless, these are exceptional cases. In the vast majority of divorces, a 50-50 split, or something close to it, is the equitable division.

Court-Ordered Property Division

When spouses wrangle over property, the court must divide it for them during a trial. According to equitable distribution, the division must be "just and reasonable" or "equitable." But since these general principles don't give enough guidance, courts have developed nine specific factors for property division:

- duration of the marriage
- contribution of the parties to the marital estate
- age of the parties
- health of the parties
- life status of the parties
- necessities and circumstances of the parties
- earning abilities of the parties
- past relations and conduct of the parties
- general principles of equity

In many states, property divisions are based solely on economic factors. If fault is taken into account, it's only to the extent that fault has had an impact on the property. For example, California ignores fault in property divisions except when one spouse has squandered the community property. In that case of "economic fault," the other spouse gets a greater share of the property.

Most of Michigan's property division factors are also economic. But fault creeps into divorce when the property division is contested through the "past relations and conduct of the parties" factor. And in Michigan, this fault isn't confined to misuse of property. It can include almost any type of marital misconduct, no matter how embarrassing or lurid.

Since equitable distribution is designed to be flexible, courts can weigh the property division factors much as they wish. They can focus on the important factors in the case, while disregarding others that don't apply. Courts may also consider other things through the catch-all "general principles of equity" factor.

Courts can avoid all that if the parties have a prenuptial agreement, since the agreement will normally control the division of property. Prenuptial agreements (also called antenuptial agreements or marital contracts) are contracts between spouses-to-be that spell out how property shall be divided when the marriage ends by death or divorce.

Michigan courts weren't always willing to use prenuptial agreements during divorce. For years, they refused to enforce these agreements believing that they encouraged divorce. But in 1991, the Michigan Court of Appeals reversed that rule and decided that prenuptial agreements are enforceable when: 1) the agreement was fairly entered into before the marriage 2) the agreement itself was fair at the time it was signed 3) facts and circumstances haven't changed enough since the agreement was signed that would make it unfair to enforce the agreement.

Uncontested Property Division

Before you and your spouse agree on a property division, you must know the extent and value of your property. "Can I Get a Fair Property Division?" on page 29 has important information about that. It tells which property is divisible in a divorce, and how to value it.

After you agree on a property division, the court should approve it because you have more control over property division than the other divorce issues. If you happen to have a prenuptial agreement dealing with divorce, you should be able to use it to divide your property, unless the agreement is "unfair" (see above for the fairness requirements for prenuptial agreements). Whatever you decide about property division, see "Property Division Provisions" in Appendix E for information about providing for and carrying out the division.

Alimony

From the start, American courts awarded support in the form of alimony to wives. In 1641, just two years after the first American divorce, Massachusetts Bay Colony passed a law giving wives a right to alimony.

During this era, courts regarded alimony as wife-support, and husbands never got it. But in the 1960s, states revised their alimony laws to make it payable to either men or women. Michigan amended its alimony law in 1970 to permit alimony for men.

Since then, there have been some well-publicized cases of women paying alimony to men. Actresses Jane Seymour and Roseanne Arnold reportedly pay their former husbands alimony. And even among the less famous, men are receiving alimony more often as women achieve financial parity with men. But typically, men are the alimony payers and women are the recipients.

Despite all the attention it gets, alimony has never been very common. At the beginning of this century, alimony was awarded in a scant 9.3% of divorces. Although figures are hard to come by, that percentage seems to have increased during the next 50 years. One study of California divorces in 1968 found that wives received alimony in 20% of divorces. But by 1975, only 14% of divorce cases included alimony.

As the number of alimony orders declined, the duration of alimony also shrank. Years ago, alimony was usually an open-ended award which continued indefinitely until the wife remarried or died. Nowadays, alimony is likely to be for a limited time—maybe a year or two—to help the recipient get back on his/her feet. This kind of short-term alimony is sometimes referred to as rehabilitative or transitional alimony.

In Michigan, alimony can be paid during a divorce or afterward. Alimony during a divorce is available as a form of temporary relief. In addition, courts will sometimes order extra alimony-like payments earmarked for specific things like house payments, rent or utilities (see "Do I Need 'Temporary Relief'?" on page 36 for more about temporary alimony and support).

Whether or not temporary alimony has been ordered, alimony can be granted in the Judgment of Divorce at the end of the divorce. In most cases, alimony takes the form of cash payments payable periodically.*

These payments will not last forever because divorce judgments invariably make alimony subject to conditions ending it. These conditions are negotiable between the spouses, but most judgments contain several of the following:

Death. Alimony almost always ends when the recipient dies (as explained below, there are sound tax reasons for making such a provision). Alimony doesn't automatically end when the payer dies, and it can survive and become a debt of his/her estate. Nevertheless, judgments often terminate alimony when payers die.

Remarriage. Alimony often ends when the recipient remarries, but seldom ends if the payer remarries.

Cohabitation. To prevent recipients from choosing cohabitation over remarriage as a way to keep alimony, the alimony may end if the recipient cohabitates with a member of the opposite sex.

Date. Alimony may end on a specific date.

Modification. In Michigan, (periodic) alimony is subject to future increase or decrease by the court when there has been a change in the parties' circumstances. This could reduce or even terminate the alimony. Michigan, unlike most states, doesn't permit nonmodifiable periodic alimony.

Types of Alimony

Alimony is a slippery word because Michigan divorce law, federal tax law and federal bankruptcy law all define it differently. Making matters worse, Michigan court rules use the phrase spousal support instead of alimony. Because of this, the forms in this book also use spousal support to mean alimony, although the text will continue to use the familiar term alimony.

Michigan divorce law regards as alimony divorce-related transfers of money or other property from one spouse to the other for purposes of support. This definition includes two types of alimony: periodic alimony and alimony-in-gross. For years, the difference between the two was that periodic alimony was subject to conditions that might end it anytime, while alimony-in-gross was a fixed and unconditional obligation. Recently, this distinction has become blurred. According to the new view, alimony-in-gross is still a fixed obligation, but like periodic alimony, it can be subject to conditions that end it.

---

*   This discussion applies only to periodic alimony, not alimony-in-gross. See below for the difference.

As the resemblance between periodic alimony and alimony-in-gross has increased, courts now look at the intent of the parties to distinguish the two. If the court is convinced that the parties wanted periodic alimony, it's periodic alimony; if they intended alimony-in-gross, it's alimony-in-gross. Under this new test, labels are important because they are the best evidence of the parties' intent. Therefore, a divorce judgment should clearly designate alimony as either periodic alimony or alimony-in-gross.

Federal law has its own rules for defining alimony. The federal tax law generally disregards what parties call their payments. Instead, it considers support payments as alimony if they are:

- paid in cash (including checks or money orders)
- made to a spouse or to someone on his/her behalf
- made in a divorce document (such as a divorce judgment)
- made when the spouses are living apart (subject to several exceptions, including payment of temporary alimony)
- end on the death of the recipient-spouse
- not provided as child support
- not designated as something other than alimony

These tax rules are important because payments that qualify as alimony get special tax treatment. The payments are deductible by the payer and counted as income for the recipient.

Federal bankruptcy law has yet another definition of alimony. According to bankruptcy law, support payments qualify as alimony if they are: 1) intended by the parties as alimony 2) actually used for support 3) a reasonable amount of support. When payments are treated as alimony under bankruptcy law, they're protected from elimination or discharge during a bankruptcy of the payer. If the payments don't qualify as alimony, the payer can sometimes discharge them in bankruptcy.

Court-Ordered Alimony

When spouses contest the issue of alimony, the court must decide the issue in a trial. To determine whether alimony is payable, the court considers the following factors:

- length of the marriage
- ability of the parties to work
- source of and amount of property awarded to the parties
- age of the parties
- ability of the parties to pay alimony
- present situation of the parties
- needs of the parties
- health of the parties

- prior standard of living of the parties and whether either is responsible for the support of others
- past relations and conduct of the parties
- general principles of equity

Like property division, the procedure for deciding alimony is flexible, so a court may apply these factors as it chooses. It can weigh the factors unequally, disregard ones that don't apply, or add others that seem important through the catch-all "general principles of equity" factor.

Most of the alimony factors are economic. That makes sense because what alimony is really about is the need of one spouse for support and the ability of the other to pay it. But fault can creep in through the "past relations and conduct of the parties" factor. As with property division, fault in contested alimony cases may include almost any evidence of marital misconduct.

After a court decides that alimony is due, it must then determine the amount. In Michigan, there are no uniform alimony guidelines as there are for child support. So most judges set alimony on a case-by-case basis using the following factors:

- length of the marriage
- contributions of the parties to the joint estate
- age and health of the parties
- parties' stations in life
- necessities of the parties
- earning ability of the parties

In 1983, Washtenaw County rejected the case-by-case approach and adopted an alimony formula. It judges the strength of an alimony claim (length of the marriage, age, income and job skills are the most important factors), adjusts the claim for other factors and then provides for a mathematical computation of alimony. Recently, other counties have begun using Washtenaw's formula or adaptations of it. This suggests a need for a uniform state-wide formula, which may be developed in the future.

Uncontested Alimony

Since alimony isn't ordered in most divorces, divorce judgments usually waive (surrender) alimony. Sometimes it's possible to reserve alimony, allowing you to ask for it after the divorce. Or you and your spouse can agree to have alimony granted by including an alimony order in your divorce judgment.

"Alimony Provisions" in Appendix E has more information about all those methods of dealing with alimony. It also includes two basic alimony orders for short- and long-term periodic alimony. If you want alimony-in-gross instead, see a lawyer for help.

Other Divorce Issues

Ending the marriage, property division and alimony are not the only divorce issues. But any other divorce issues are relatively minor and seldom contested.

Name change for women is one such minor issue. After a divorce, women often want to drop their married names and resume their maiden or former names. For them, Michigan law offers two name change methods: 1) common law name change 2) court-ordered name change from: (a) the court when the divorce is granted (b) a separate name change case later.

The common law method is the easiest because all you do is choose a new name and begin using it regularly. No court order is necessary. The name change is legal as long as you're not adopting a new name for a fraudulent or improper purpose.

The trouble with a common law name change is that others may not always recognize it. As a result, most women choose formal court-ordered name changes.

It's easy for a woman to change her name during divorce. When the divorce is final, the court can allow the wife, whether she is plaintiff or defendant, to adopt a different surname (last name). She may resume a maiden or former name, or choose any other surname. The only restriction is that the name change mustn't be sought with "any fraudulent or evil intent" (to avoid past debts, hide from law enforcement officials, etc.). The divorce papers in this book have provisions for women to ask for and receive name changes.

Some women who ultimately want to change their names aren't ready for name changes during divorce. For personal or other reasons, they may want to keep their married names for a while, and then change later.

Women seeking name changes post-divorce must file separate name change cases. Before filing, they must satisfy a one-year county residency requirement. They must be fingerprinted by the police and submit to a criminal background check. After publishing a legal notice in the newspaper, they must attend a court hearing to get the name change.

Needless to say, this procedure takes much more effort than a divorce name change. That's why most women, if they have a choice, choose a name change during divorce.

At this time, men aren't allowed to change their names during divorce, as women can. Until the law changes, men must file separate name change cases, outside of divorce, for court-ordered name changes.

PART III: Doing an Uncontested Divorce Yourself

Most uncontested divorces go smoothly. But divorce remains a difficult legal procedure, and can sometimes get complicated. There may be a problem with jurisdiction, trouble serving the divorce papers, difficulty dividing the property, or the danger of spouse abuse. All these problems and more may make your divorce—although it's uncontested—too difficult for you to do yourself.

Am I Married?

It may seem silly, but the first thing you should do before a divorce is make sure you are really married. If you discover that you aren't married, you won't need a divorce to split up.

The legality of a marriage is judged by the law of where it began, not where it ends. If you were married in Michigan, you look at Michigan marriage law. Those married out of state must consider the marriage law of that place.

Michigan authorizes two types of marriage: 1) ceremonial marriage, performed by most clergymen and some government officials 2) secret marriage, a rather obscure form of marriage before a probate judge for the benefit of: (a) people with a good reason to keep their marriage secret (b) children under the age of 16 in certain circumstances. Other states have different types of ceremonial marriage.

Most states have abolished common law marriage, in which couples informally agree to live together as husband and wife. However, many states had it in the past. Michigan recognized common law marriage until January

1, 1957. Today, only the District of Columbia and the following states permit common law marriage:

- Alabama
- Colorado
- Georgia
- Idaho
- Iowa
- Kansas
- Montana

- Oklahoma
- Pennsylvania
- Rhode Island
- South Carolina
- Texas
- Utah

If your common law marriage began in one of these states, it's legal in Michigan. Or if it began in Michigan before January 1, 1957, or in other states while they recognized the institution, it's also valid here.

If you doubt whether you are really married, check with the official of the office where you believe your marriage license is filed. In Michigan, that official is the county clerk who issued the license to you; in other states it might be someone else. Another way to trace marriage records is through a state vital records office. Every state has an office that compiles records of marriages, divorces, births and deaths. By writing to the vital records office of the state in which you think you were married, you can get a copy of your marriage license, if one exists.

After you confirm that you are married, you should also make sure that your marriage hasn't previously ended by divorce or annulment. Unlike common law marriage, there is no such thing as informal "common law" divorce. So despite what some people think, tearing up your marriage license, giving back wedding rings, etc. will not make you divorced. Therefore, any divorce that your spouse may have gotten must have been court-ordered.

If you think that you may have been involved in a prior divorce, investigate and see whether a divorce judgment (also known as a decree or order in some states) was ever issued in the case. The court where the divorce was filed will have record of the judgment. If you don't have much information about the divorce, use the procedure described above to contact the vital records office of the state where the divorce was filed. It should have a record of the divorce judgment, if in fact one was issued.

Naturally, your spouse's death also ends your marriage. You might not know about this if you've separated from your spouse and remained out of touch. If you suspect that your spouse has died, you can confirm that by checking to see if a death certificate was filed. In Michigan, death certificates are filed with the county clerk of the place of death. If you don't know the county, use the state vital records office.

It's also possible to have your spouse legally declared dead after a long disappearance. Like most states, Michigan has an Enoch Arden law (so called after the shipwrecked sailor of the Tennyson poem who returned from

---

More Information

To obtain Michigan marriage, divorce and death records, contact Michigans vital records office:

Michigan Department of Public Health
Office of State Registrar
P.O. Box 30195
Lansing, MI 48909
(517) 335-8655

To find vital records offices in other states, order the booklet "Where to Write for Vital Records" (#143C), by sending a $2.25 check (payable to "Superintendent of Documents"), to:

R. Woods
Consumer Information Center -GC
P.O. Box 100
Pueblo, CO 81002

ten years at sea to find his wife remarried), which allows a person to be declared dead after seven years of complete absence.

Do I Really Want to End My Marriage?

When you get a divorce, the marriage between you and your spouse is ended finally and irrevocably. This allows each of you to remarry, if you wish. As someone considering divorce, you are probably well aware of these and other benefits of divorce.

But as you prepare to divorce, don't forget the advantages of remaining married. Marriage offers many valuable rights, such as: 1) support 2) property rights 3) estate and will rights 4) private benefits 5) public benefits 6) miscellaneous rights.

To be sure, some of these rights can be continued or compensated after a divorce. You can sometimes get postdivorce support in the form of alimony, and your property rights, including rights in retirement plans, can be recovered in the property division of the divorce.

But many marital rights are lost forever by a divorce. After a divorce, you lose all rights to your spouse's estate, including: 1) the right to a share of his/her estate if s/he dies without a will 2) the right to elect against your spouse's will (to get a minimum share of the estate if the will slights you) 3) dower (an estate that widows have in their husbands' real property) 4) homestead (the right to live in the marital home after your spouse's death 5) miscellaneous allowances from your deceased spouse's estate. Divorce also automatically revokes all distributions of property and some appointments in your spouse's will benefiting you.

You may also lose valuable private benefits available through your spouse, such as retirement, fringe, life and health insurance benefits. With medical costs increasing rapidly, losing health insurance is risky, particularly for those who are medically uninsurable but unable to qualify for public coverage. A 1985 law, the Consolidated Omnibus Budget Reconciliation Act, or COBRA for short, tries to correct this problem by requiring larger employers (with 20 or more employees) to offer health insurance to their employees' ex-spouses (and dependent children) at group rates for up to three years. This is an important guarantee for families. It's especially valuable for a medically uninsurable ex-spouse, since COBRA says that health coverage must be offered without regard to medical insurability.

The death of your spouse after your divorce will leave you without public benefits, such as wrongful death claims or survivor's benefits from worker's compensation or no-fault automobile insurance, that you might have enjoyed had you remained married. What's worse, if you happen to

---

More Information

On divorce and social security, get "A Woman's Guide to Social Security" from your local social security office.

About obtaining health insurance through COBRA, send a SASE to:

Insurance Continuation
Older Women's League (OWL)
666 11th St. N.W.
Suite 700
Washington, DC 20001

See "Can I Get A Fair Property Division?" on page 29 for resources about retirement benefits.

Good information about these and other topics:

The Dollars and Sense of Divorce, Judith Briles, New York: MasterMedia, 1988

Divorce & Money, Violet Woodhouse and Victoria Felton-Collins, Berkeley: Nolo Press, 1996

divorce before the tenth anniversary of your marriage, you may lose the right to get social security benefits based on your spouse's earnings record.

Divorce also jeopardizes other miscellaneous marital rights that you may have never thought about. For example, noncitizen immigrants can lose entrance or residency rights when they divorce U.S. citizens. After a divorce, you cannot file a joint income tax return, and may face a bigger tax bill. Marriage also entitles you to discounts on airplane tickets, hotels, etc., which single people don't have.

After considering all that marriage offers, you may decide that it isn't so bad after all. If you think that your marriage can be saved, you may find marriage counseling helpful. Many religious and human service organizations provide counseling, usually without charge. The circuit courts in some counties have marriage counseling available or give referrals. You can find private marriage counselors listed in the yellow pages under "Marriage and Family Counselors." Or call the American Association for Marriage and Family Therapy at 1-800-374-2638 for a list of private marriage counselors in your area. These private marriage counselors charge fees for their services, but some health insurance policies pay for the cost.

Is Divorce the Best Way to End My Marriage?

Divorce isn't the only remedy for a bad marriage. By declaring a marriage nonexistent, an annulment also ends the marriage. A legal separation—known as separate maintenance in Michigan—ends a marital relationship, although the marriage itself is left intact. Like a divorce, an annulment or separate maintenance allows the court to decide the issues of property division and alimony. Before you embark on a divorce, determine if an annulment or separate maintenance would be better for you.

Annulment

Many people find annulments confusing. For one thing, they often mix up legal annulments with religious annulments. Legal annulments are granted by courts of law, and affect one's legal rights. Some religious denominations, notably the Roman Catholic Church, offer religious annulments. These end marriages in the eyes in the church, restoring various religious privileges. A religious annulment is obtained from the religious organization and has absolutely no effect on legal rights.

Another misunderstanding about annulments is that they are routinely available for spouses who have been married for a short time and simply want to "call the whole thing off." The fact is, the length of a marriage is often insignificant: A marriage of a few days may not be annullable, just as a marriage of many years can be annulled. The real distinction between divorce and annulment is that a divorce ends a valid marriage, while an annulment is a legal declaration that no marriage ever existed because of a serious legal defect in the marriage at the time it was performed.

Like most states, Michigan presumes that marriages are legally valid. As a result, minor legal defects in a marriage, such as irregularities in the marriage ceremony, lack of authority of the person who performed the ceremony, etc., are not grounds for annulment. But if the legal defect is serious, the marriage is subject to annulment. In Michigan, the serious legal defects providing grounds for an annulment concern whether the spouses: 1) had the legal capacity to marry 2) properly consented to marriage.*

> # Glossary
>
> *Divorce*–legal procedure that ends a marriage.
>
> *Annulment*–says that a marriage is legally defective and never really existed.
>
> *Separate maintenance*–like a legal separation, allowing spouses to live apart with marriage still intact.

Legal capacity. One must satisfy several requirements to marry in Michigan. If a spouse failed to meet any of these requirements when the marriage was performed, the spouse lacked the legal capacity for marriage. This defect can provide grounds for annulment:

¶ *Bigamy.* A spouse marries while already married to someone else.

¶ Incest. The spouses are related too closely by blood (you cannot marry a parent, child, grandchild, grandparent, brother or sister, aunt or uncle, niece or nephew or first cousin) or marriage (a stepparent, stepchild, stepgrandchild, son- or daughter-in-law, father- or mother-in-law, spouse of a grandchild or grandparent-in-law are all not marriageable).

¶ *Same-sex marriage.* Michigan doesn't permit same sex marriage, or recognize same-sex marriages from other states.

¶ *Underage.* Eighteen is the age of consent to marry in Michigan. Men and women 16-18 can marry if they obtain the proper parental consent. Under some circumstances, children under 16 can marry with parental consent in a secret marriage in probate court. Anyone who marries while underage and/or without the proper parental consent, lacks the legal capacity to marry.

¶ *Mental incompetency.* Mental incompetency of a spouse at the time of a marriage is an additional legal incapacity. Onset of mental incompetency after marriage doesn't affect the marriage.

---

*   As mentioned before, the legality of a marriage is judged by the law of the state where it began. These annulment grounds apply to Michigan marriages only. There may be different annulment grounds for out-of-state marriages.

¶ *Venereal disease.* Infection with an uncured venereal disease (syphilis or gonorrhea) at the time of the marriage is an additional type of legal incapacity.

¶ *Physical incapacity.* Sterility and some kinds of sexual dysfunction, which exist at the time of the marriage, are also recognized as incapacities.

Consent. According to Michigan law, both spouses must give proper consent to their marriage. If a spouse's consent is absent or defective, for any of the reasons below, the marriage may be annulled:

¶ *Force.* A spouse's consent to the marriage is obtained forcibly. Ordinarily, the force must be the use or threat of physical force, but in some cases extreme psychological duress will qualify as force.

¶ *Intoxication.* A spouse's consent to the marriage might be defective if s/he is under the influence of alcohol or drugs when the marriage is performed.

¶ *Fraud.* Fraud is a misrepresentation that causes someone to do something. If fraud is used to obtain consent to a marriage, the fraud can invalidate the marriage. Michigan law is clear that the fraud must affect an essential part of the marriage. For example, a spouse's misrepresentation about his/her ability to have or want children, or about an intention to engage in cohabitation or sexual relations, may be important enough to annul the marriage. But misrepresentations by a spouse about character, wealth, family background or premarital life don't provide fraud grounds for an annulment.

More Information

About Michigan marriage, request the pamphlet "Manual on Michigan Marriage Law," from:

State Bar of Michigan
Family Law Section
306 Townsend St.
Lansing, MI 48933

¶ *Sham marriage.* Even when consent to a marriage is given voluntarily and knowingly, the consent might be defective if it wasn't seriously intended. Marriages based on such false consent are regarded as sham marriages, making them subject to annulment. An example of a sham marriage is a marriage by an immigrant who marries a U.S. citizen solely to obtain permanent residency in this country. In that case, the immigrant's marriage may appear to be proper, but it is really nothing more than a ruse to obtain residency in this country.

If you possess any of these grounds for annulment, you may be able to end your marriage by annulment. Or you can disregard the annulment grounds, file for divorce and end your marriage that way. Which is the better choice?

There is no simple answer to this question because divorces closely resemble annulments. Both procedures end marriages and free spouses to remarry. They both divide property. But alimony, especially long-term alimony, is difficult to get in an annulment.

An annulment may be quicker than a divorce. Annulments don't have waiting periods as divorces do (see "How Long Will My Divorce Take?" on page 27 for information about divorce waiting periods). And there are no state or county residency requirements for annulments as there are in divorce cases (see "Can I Get a Divorce in Michigan?" and "Can I File the Divorce in My County?" on pages 24-26 for more on state and county divorce residency requirements).

On the other hand, the grounds for annulment are harder to prove and easier to defend against than the no-fault divorce grounds. What's worse, most annulment grounds are based on fault. This means that an annulment can be messy, like divorce was under the old fault law.

If you believe that you have grounds for an annulment and cannot decide whether to file for divorce or annulment, talk with a lawyer about which procedure to use. Act quickly because it's possible to lose annulment grounds by waiting too long. If you decide to seek an annulment, have the lawyer represent you because this book doesn't have instructions or forms for annulment.

Separation

Unlike divorce or annulment, separation doesn't end a marriage. It merely ends the marital relationship between the spouses, leaving the marriage itself intact. Despite that fact, there may be sound reasons for choosing separation over divorce or annulment.

Years ago, people often separated to avoid the social stigma of divorce. With divorce more common, this stigma has faded. Nevertheless, some people may still want to separate and remain married for social or religious reasons.

Some couples choose separation for more practical reasons. As explained before, spouses can lose valuable marital rights when their marriage ends. Since separation doesn't break the legal bond of marriage, it preserves these marital rights. With this in mind, spouses may decide to separate temporarily, and divorce later when losing these rights is not so important. For example, spouses married eight or nine years might agree to separate for a few years, and then divorce, so they can qualify for social security benefits based on each other's earnings under the ten-year rule mentioned above. Or they may remain married to preserve benefits like health insurance.

You don't need to go to court to separate. As a matter of fact, spouses can separate informally and live apart indefinitely. Separated spouses usually work out arrangements for property division and sometimes alimony. To avoid disputes, some estranged spouses enter into written separation or settlement agreements. These agreements spell out how property division and alimony are handled during the separation. In addition, the agreement can settle these issues for any divorce following the separation.

An informal separation—even one with a written separation agreement—is difficult to maintain. If the spouses disagree about something, they have no place to resolve their dispute. As a result, some separated spouses seek a formal, court-ordered separation, which is popularly known as a legal separation.

Michigan law provides for a special type of legal separation called separate maintenance. Separate maintenance doesn't end the marriage. But it settles the issues of property division and alimony while the spouses live apart.

The procedure for getting a separate maintenance is like that for a divorce. Even the same no-fault grounds are used. Despite the resemblance, it's much harder to get a separate maintenance because Michigan law allows a defendant in a separate maintenance case to ask for a divorce instead. After such a request, the court must grant the divorce if the marriage has permanently broken down. Therefore, it's impossible to get a separate maintenance without the consent of the other spouse. All this makes separate maintenance difficult, so see a lawyer if you want one.

Can I Get a Divorce in Michigan?

After deciding that a divorce is what you want, you must then determine whether you can get one in Michigan. Not everyone is entitled to divorce in Michigan. To get a divorce in this state, Michigan courts must have jurisdiction to hear your divorce case.

Michigan divorce jurisdiction is based on the past and present residences of the spouses. These residences determine whether there is either full or limited jurisdiction for the case. A court can take full jurisdiction when at least the defendant-spouse is residing in Michigan (the plaintiff-spouse may be residing here as well), or when the spouses resided together in Michigan at some time during their marriage. Limited jurisdiction is present when only the plaintiff-spouse resides in Michigan and the defendant never resided here with him/her during their marriage.

Glossary

Plaintiff–spouse who files for divorce.

Defendant–spouse whom divorce is filed against.

Jurisdiction–power of a court to decide a divorce case.

Like other states, Michigan also imposes a residency requirement on divorce to discourage migratory divorce. In Michigan, the residency period is 180 days.

The chart on the opposite page depicts Michigan divorce jurisdiction with the residency requirement added. As difficult as it is, jurisdiction is important because it determines how much of your case the court can decide. As explained in Part II, divorce is divisible into several issues: end of marriage, property division and alimony. For reasons that are too complicated to explain here, certain divorce issues may need a particular type of jurisdiction. For example, property division and alimony require full jurisdiction, while ending a marriage can use either limited or full jurisdiction.

When a court has full jurisdiction, it can do a divorce completely. It can end the marriage, divide the property and award alimony. With only limited jurisdiction, a court can end the marriage, but it cannot decide property division or alimony.

Divorces with minor children almost always require full jurisdiction. But divorces without minor children can sometimes get by with limited jurisdiction. If you have little property, and don't seek alimony, limited jurisdic-

Michigan Divorce Jurisdiction

	Defendant is a Michigan resident (and has been for at least 180 days immediately before the divorce is filed)	Defendant once resided with plaintiff in Michigan during their marriage, then moved out of state	Defendant never resided with plaintiff in Michigan during their marriage
Plaintiff is a Michigan resident (and has been for at least 180 days immediately before the divorce is filed)	Full jurisdiction immediately*	Full jurisdiction immediately**	Limited jurisdiction immediately**
Plaintiff once resided with defendant in Michigan during their marriage, then moved out of state	Full jurisdiction immediately	No jurisdiction until plaintiff (or defendant) moves back to Michigan and has resided here at least 180 days immediately before the divorce is filed, then full jurisdiction**	
Plaintiff never resided with defendant in Michigan during their marriage	Full jurisdiction immediately		No jurisdiction until plaintiff (or defendant) moves to Michigan and has resided here at least 180 days immediately before the divorce is filed, then only limited jurisdiction**

* In fact, *either* plaintiff or defendant can satisfy the 180-day residency requirement by having resided in Michigan at least 180 days immediately before the divorce is filed.

** Full jurisdiction can also be obtained on a nonresident defendant by serving him/her while present in Michigan, such as during a visit to the state.

tion may be enough. If not, contact a lawyer to see about getting full Michigan jurisdiction or filing for divorce in the defendant's state.

Residency is vital to your case as the basis for jurisdiction. But what is it really? Residency has several different legal meanings. For the purposes of divorce, residency means living in a place with the intention of remaining there. In other words, it's physical habitation in a place plus the mental state of intending to stay there.

Long-time residents of Michigan don't have to worry about residency. But if you've moved to the state recently, you can establish residency by: 1) registering to vote here 2) getting a Michigan driver's license 3) owning property in the state (it's even better if you file for a homestead property tax exemption at your Michigan address) 4) working and filing Michigan income tax returns.

Once established in Michigan, residency isn't lost by temporary absences out of state, such as vacations or business trips. Nor is it disturbed by leaving the state under military or government orders. For example, a resident of Michigan who enters the U.S. military or foreign service remains a Michigan resident during active duty wherever assigned.

Residency may be important for the purposes of jurisdiction before you file a divorce, but it's much less important afterward. In fact, after you file the divorce you or your spouse can move anywhere—in or outside Michigan—without losing jurisdiction for your divorce.

Can I File the Divorce in My County?

Assuming Michigan courts have some type of jurisdiction for your divorce, you must then file in the Michigan county with proper venue. In divorce cases, venue exists in the court where either you or your spouse has resided at least 10 days immediately before the divorce is filed.

Naturally, when you both reside in the same county, the divorce must be filed there. But when you reside in different Michigan counties,* venue is proper in either county. For the sake of convenience, most people choose to file in their own counties.

Incidentally, residency for venue purposes is a place of permanent habitation, just as it is for jurisdiction. Prisoners are presumed to remain residents of the counties they resided in before imprisonment. However, prisoners can become residents of the counties of their imprisonment if they can prove they intend to reside there after release. This allows them to file for divorce where they are imprisoned.

Can My Spouse Be Served with the Divorce Papers?

Regardless of the type of jurisdiction for a divorce, the defendant must get notice of the divorce. Like other lawsuits, notice in divorce cases is provided by serving the initial divorce papers upon defendants. Service is explained in detail in Chapter 2. At this point, you should know that service is easy and cheap if your spouse is available to receive the divorce papers. In that case, you can obtain service by any of three methods: 1) acknowledgment 2) mail 3) delivery. It doesn't matter where your spouse lives, because these service methods can be used anywhere in or outside Michigan.

Service can be difficult if a defendant is elusive (you know where the defendant is, but s/he is eluding or avoiding you). It's even more difficult if the defendant has disappeared (you don't know the whereabouts of the

---

*   If the defendant resides out of state, venue will be in the Michigan county where the plaintiff resides. In those few cases with out-of-state plaintiffs, venue will be in the Michigan county where the defendant resides.

defendant). Luckily, the court rules provide for forms of alternate service to give hard-to-find defendants some type of notice (Appendix B has more about obtaining alternate service on elusive or disappeared defendants). Thanks to this wide choice of service methods, you can be assured that when there is jurisdiction for your divorce there will be a way to serve the defendant.

What If My Spouse or I Am in the Military Service?

Divorcing a spouse in the U.S. military service poses special problems. There are practical problems of finding and serving divorce papers on the defendant-military spouse, who may be stationed at a far-flung military base.

There is also a federal law—the Soldiers' and Sailors' Civil Relief Act (SSCRA)—protecting *active-duty* servicepersons in the Army, Navy, Air Force, Marine Corps, Coast Guard and National Guard from lawsuits, including divorces. The SSCRA doesn't necessarily rule out divorces for servicepersons. The act allows a divorce to go through when the serviceperson's ability to respond to the divorce is "not materially affected" by his/her military service.

The SSCRA protects both plaintiffs and defendants. If you are a plaintiff-serviceperson, you can waive the act's protection and get a divorce without worrying about the act. If you were a Michigan resident before enlistment, you're still a Michigan resident wherever you may be stationed as servicepersons normally keep their pre-enlistment state residency. Your Michigan residency will provide a basis for jurisdiction and venue in the state. It's true that your divorce will be a little difficult to manage if you're stationed out of state. But you can file your divorce papers by mail. And you can obtain leave to attend the final hearing at the end of the divorce.

Things are much more complicated if the defendant is an active-duty serviceperson. To satisfy the SSCRA, you must show that the defendant has the ability to respond to the divorce despite his/her military service. This is difficult to do. That's why you should seek legal assistance if your spouse is in active-duty military service.

How Long Will My Divorce Take?

Uncontested divorces take longer to complete than most uncontested lawsuits because Michigan law imposes two statutory waiting periods on divorces:

- 60 days in cases without minor children
- six months in cases with minor children

The waiting periods serve to delay divorces. The chief reason for the delay is to give the parties a chance to cool off, and possibly reconcile, after the heat of the divorce filing has passed.

In your case, the 60-day statutory waiting period applies. This means that at least 60 days must elapse between the day you file your divorce and the day you finish it in court at the final hearing.

In addition to the statutory waiting period, there may also be unpredictable court-caused delays. Some courts are very busy and may not be able to hear your divorce immediately after the statutory waiting period expires. As a result, your divorce will take at least 60 days, and maybe a while longer if the court is busy.

How Much Will My Divorce Cost?

Doing your own divorce saves you lawyer fees, but not the court fees of the case. These court fees are due in all divorces—with or without lawyers. The court fees for uncontested divorces without minor children include:

Filing fee. The current fee for filing a divorce is $100. The legislature may increase the filing and other fees sometime during the next few years, although nothing has been scheduled yet.

Service fee. You can expect to pay $0-30 to have the divorce papers served. The amount of the service fee depends on the method of service you use. Service by acknowledgment is usually available for free. Service by mail is around $6. Service by delivery is usually $16-30. If you use a sheriff for service by delivery, the sheriff charges a $16 fee, plus mileage to and from the defendant. Commercial process servers' fees for service by delivery may be slightly higher.

Motion fee. You must pay a $20 fee whenever you file a motion. You probably won't need to file any motions in your uncontested divorce case, unless you have to ask for something extraordinary, like alternate service.

Excluding a service fee, your court fees should be $100 (the current filing fee). Add to that a service fee, which depends on the method of service used.

Thanks to a landmark U.S. Supreme Court decision, poor people don't have to pay these court fees. In *Boddie v. Connecticut*, the supreme court decided that states must give everyone access to divorce, since they alone have the power to grant divorces. This means that those who can't afford divorce court fees are entitled to exemptions from payment. After the *Boddie* decision in 1971, Michigan adopted a uniform fee exemption procedure for all types of cases, including divorce. See Appendix A for information about qualifying and applying for a fee exemption.

Do I Have Minor Children in My Divorce?

To get a divorce without minor children, you mustn't have any "divorce children" (children under the age of 18 on the day you file for divorce). Since you obtained this edition of *The Michigan Divorce Book*, you obviously believe

Divorce Children

	Minor children included in divorce	Comments/exceptions
Children born during plaintiff's and defendant's present marriage	Yes	But paternity of children born during a marriage can be disproved by strong evidence that the father is not really the father. If paternity is disproved, the child would usually not be included in the divorce.
Unborn children of the marriage	Yes	
Children born during a previous marriage of plaintiff and defendant	Yes	
Children born to plaintiff and defendant outside of their marriage	Yes, if...	Paternity has been established before the divorce or if it can be proved during the divorce.
Children *legally* adopted by plaintiff and defendant during their marriage	Yes	
Stepchildren of plaintiff or defendant	No	But if a stepchild was adopted by plaintiff or defendant in a stepparent adoption, it will be a legally adopted child of theirs.
Children given up for adoption, or children over whom both plaintiff and defendant have lost parental rights	No	But if only one parent has lost parental rights, include the children in the divorce and explain the circumstances of the parent's loss of parental rights.

that you don't have any divorce children. But before you make this assumption, see the chart above defining divorce children.

If you do have divorce children, you must use a different divorce procedure for cases with minor children. You may be able to use *The Michigan Divorce Book (with minor children)* to do the divorce. See the order form at the front of the book for ordering information.

Can I Get a Fair Property Division?

As explained in "Property Division" on page 9, you are entitled to an equitable division of your property in a divorce. But exactly which property is subject to division?

Some states have rigid schemes for dividing property in divorces. They classify property as either marital/community property or nonmarital/separate property. In these states, only marital/community property is divisible during divorce.

In Michigan, by contrast, divorce property division is more flexible. Everything the spouses own is potentially subject to division. Despite what many people believe, this may include property the spouses brought into their marriage. It can also reach inheritances, will gifts or other gifts (including wedding gifts) received before or during the marriage.

Ordinarily, premarital property, inheritances and gifts are left out of divorce property division, and the spouse who owns this property keeps it. But the nonowner-spouse may claim a share of this property when: 1) s/he or the parties' children need the property for support 2) s/he has contributed to "acquisition, improvement or accumulation" of the property.

Saying that all property is potentially divisible in a divorce begs the question of what is property? Does it include everything the spouses possess, or only those things with a definite market value?

Ten or twenty years ago, almost everyone agreed that property for divorce purposes was confined to real property (land and buildings) and personal property, such as cash, bank accounts, stocks, bonds, household goods, tools, motor vehicles, etc., with a definite market value. But over the last decade, the definition of property has steadily expanded to include almost anything of value, regardless of whether it has a market value. So besides the familiar old property that has always been divided in divorces, there are several types of "new" property that may also be divisible:

Retirement benefits. For years, courts refused to divide retirement benefits, such as pensions, despite the fact that these benefits are often the most valuable thing spouses own. Over the last 20 years, courts realized the unfairness of that position and now nearly all states permit the division of pensions and other retirement benefits.

Today, Michigan courts divide almost any type of retirement benefit provided by public- or private-sector employers, including pensions, 401(k), profit-sharing, employee stock ownership (ESOP), and saving/thrift plans. Also divisible are individual retirement benefits, such as individual retirement arrangement (IRA), simplified employee pension (SEP) and Keogh (HR-10) plans. The only type of retirement benefit immune from division is social security because it already has a built-in means of paying benefits to divorced spouses (see "Do I Really Want to End My Marriage?" on page 19 for more about obtaining social security based on your spouse's earnings record).

More Information

About retirement benefits, send $23.95 for *Your Pension Rights at Divorce: What Women Need to Know* to:

Pension Rights Center
918 16th St. N.W.
Suite 704
Washington, DC 20006

Employee benefits. Employees are often eligible for valuable fringe benefits, such as health insurance, sick and vacation pay, expense accounts, club memberships, meal allowances, lodging, discounts, etc. Some of these benefits, such as banked sick and vacation pay, have been divided in divorce cases in Michigan.

Life insurance. Life insurance is often overlooked during property division, but it's divisible if it has a cash value. Whole life insurance policies usually have a cash value; term insurance policies ordinarily don't.

Businesses. Businesses, such as a sole proprietorship (one-person business) or an interest in a partnership or a small corporation whose stock is not traded publicly, are also divorce property.

Education. Michigan was one of the first states to include education in divorce property divisions. According to Michigan law, education leading to an *advanced* degree (graduate, law, medicine, etc.) is divisible when the degree was the result of a "concerted family effort." What this means is that the nondegree-spouse contributed financial or other support to the degree-spouse while s/he got the advanced degree. If so, the nondegree-spouse's contribution can be valued and awarded to him/her.

Legal claims. Some legal claims that a spouse has against third parties, such as personal injury or workers' compensation claims, are property that can be divided in divorces. For example, in one Michigan case a husband was awarded $700,000 for a libel claim, and the divorce court ruled that his wife was entitled to about half of the money.

Spouses may also have legal claims against each other that can be decided in a divorce. At one time, it was impossible for spouses to sue each other for personal injuries. This immunity has recently been abolished and spouses are adding personal injury claims to divorces with more frequency.

Debts. Although it's hard to think of debts as property, they should be weighed during the property division because debts influence the overall fairness of the division.

Whether your property is old, new or a mixture of both, you must have a good grasp of the extent and value of your property. Otherwise, you and your spouse risk agreeing to an inequitable property division. In all, you should do three things before you agree to a property division: 1) *inventory* your property 2) *value* it 3) find a way to *divide* it.

Inventorying Property

Property division begins with a complete inventory of all the property you and your spouse own. Ordinarily, only property owned when the divorce is filed will be divided. Property transferred before the divorce* or acquired during the divorce is normally left out of the division. So take your inventory just before you file.

---

* But see "Does My Property Need Protection?" on page 34 for how courts can stop a spouse from deliberately transferring property to keep it out of the divorce.

As you inventory your property, you may find that you don't know very much about it. In many marriages, one spouse handles the finances, leaving the other spouse in the dark. Luckily, there are several informal ways to get the financial information you need for the inventory.

Start with documents around the house, such as bank statements, bank books, paycheck stubs and retirement plan booklets. If you and your spouse have a joint safe deposit box, go through the box. You might find deeds, land contracts, stocks, bonds and life insurance policies hidden in the box.

Your recent joint personal tax returns, especially any schedules attached to these returns, can reveal valuable information about real property (schedules D and E) bank accounts (schedule B), and businesses (schedules C and F). Likewise, joint business income tax returns have important information about businesses. If you have discarded these returns, you can order copies by submitting Form 4506 to your IRS filing center.

Have you and your spouse applied for a loan recently? If so, you probably prepared a financial statement as part of the loan application. Since federal law makes it a crime to submit false information in the statement, it can be a reliable source of financial information.

If these informal methods fail to give you the financial information you need, there is a formal fact-finding device called discovery. Discovery comes in several forms, including depositions (oral interrogation out of court), interrogatories (written questions) and requests for documents. All these discovery methods are available during divorce to get you the financial information you need. The trouble is, discovery is difficult for nonlawyers to use. If you think you need it, contact a lawyer for help.

Valuing Property

There are many methods of valuing property. Michigan law doesn't say which method must be used, but fair market value seems to be the accepted measure of value.

Fair market value is usually defined as the price property would bring in a sale between a willing buyer and willing seller. When the property is subject to a debt, an adjustment may be necessary. For indebted property, the equity value of the property—its fair market value minus the debt against it—is often used instead of gross fair market value.

You should be able to establish the fair market value of most kinds of personal property informally without going to the trouble and expense of getting formal appraisals. To value real property, you can either: 1) compare your property to the sale prices of other similar property sold recently in your neighborhood 2) double the amount of your property's tax assessment, since assessments are usually around 50% of market value.

Cash or near-cash assets (bank accounts, certificates of deposit, money market funds, etc.) are worth their present account balances. You can estimate the value of household goods and tools by comparing them to similar used items.

The value of motor vehicles can be obtained from National Automobile Dealer Association (NADA) bluebooks. There are also price guides for stamps, coins, jewelry and antiques. The value of stocks, corporate bonds and other securities are listed daily in the *Wall Street Journal.*

Use the current redemption value for series E/EE U.S. savings bonds, and the face or par value for H/HH bonds. You can value whole life insurance by figuring the cash surrender value on the policy chart, or by asking the insurance company or your insurance agent for this value.

If these resources don't provide accurate valuations of your property, you can always get formal appraisals. There are appraisers who are competent to value many types of property and specialists who appraise only one type of property. People who buy and sell property, such as automobile or antique dealers, can also give appraisals. To find an appraiser, look in the yellow pages under "Appraisers," or call the American Society of Appraisers at 1-800-272-8258 for a certified appraiser near you.

The valuation of some new property, such as retirement benefits and businesses, poses special problems. These things have value, but there is no marketplace for them in which their value can be fixed. After all, you can't very well sell your pension to someone else. You may be able to sell a small business, but often the market is faulty and you won't get what it's really worth. Despite these problems, there are ways to assign value to new property so that it can be divided in divorce cases.

Before you can value retirement benefits, you must know what kind of benefit it is. There are two basic kinds of plans providing retirement benefits:

Defined benefit plan. In a defined benefit plan, or pension plan, the employer promises to pay a fixed amount of money as the retirement benefit. Benefits are paid by formulas taking into account the employee's age, years of service and earnings.

What an employee with a defined benefit plan has is the employer's promise of benefits; there is no retirement account reserved for the employee. Instead, the employer's retirement contributions (typically only the employer contributes) are pooled in the a common fund, and retirement benefits are drawn from the fund as needed.

Most large private- and public-sector employers have defined benefit plans, although many are now discontinuing them in favor of defined contributions plans, especially the popular 401(K) plan.

Defined contribution plan. In some ways, a defined contribution plan is the opposite of a defined benefit plan. With a defined contribution plan, the employer's contributions, instead of the retirement benefits, are fixed. Each employee has a separate retirement account earmarked for him/her, to which s/he may contribute. The money in the employee's retirement account is invested (usually by the employer), and any investment income is added to the account. At retirement, benefits are paid from the account as the employee directs.

There are many types of defined contributions plans: 401(k), profit-sharing, ESOP and saving/thrift plans (provided by employers), and IRA, SEP and Keogh (HR-10) plans (individual plans). Typically, small businesses have defined contributions plans, although the giant TIAA-CREF (the Teachers Insurance and Annuity Account-College Retirement Equity Fund), which provides retirement benefits to public school teachers, is a defined contribution plan.

The value of a defined benefit plan lies in the benefits the plan will pay in the future. These future benefits can be reduced to a current lump-sum value, called present value. Figuring present value isn't easy, but an accountant or pension specialist can do it for you. Accountants or other financial specialists can also help you value businesses or other types of new property.

To value a defined contribution plan, you simply take the current account balance. You can get this figure from a recent benefit statement or by requesting it from the retirement plan administrator.

Dividing Property

All real property must be divided by separate property division provisions in the divorce judgment. Some personal property, including valuable things like motor vehicles and new property (retirement benefits, businesses, etc.) must also be divided individually. But you can divide most personal property, such as household goods, clothing and personal items, by just splitting it up. "Property Division Provisions" in Appendix E has more information and sample provisions for all kinds of property divisions.

Does My Property Need Protection?

Divorce sometimes puts property at risk. Spouses may try to transfer property to others, before or during the divorce, to keep it out of the property division. If the divorce is bitter, spouses may take out their frustrations on the property. A while ago, a Macomb County woman got back at her husband by destroying his collection of rare Frank Sinatra records (when Sinatra read about the incident he graciously offered to replace some of the discs). But that's nothing compared to a Seattle husband who, to spite his wife, took a bulldozer and demolished their $90,000 house!

Michigan courts have the power to prevent this kind of mischief. They can issue orders protecting property from transfer or destruction. Regrettably, this book doesn't have the instructions and forms to get these orders, so see a lawyer if you need one.

Debts can also jeopardize property and wealth during divorce. Financial stability often breaks down amid a divorce, as spouses are tempted to run up debts on joint accounts. Both spouses are liable for these joint debts regardless of which spouse incurred them. Thus, it's a good idea to close or at least freeze all joint accounts (credit card, charge accounts, etc.), if possible, immediately after separation.

You can close a joint account quickly if no debts remain in the account. If debts exist, you can pay these off or sometimes transfer them to individual accounts. Another option is to freeze the account, so no new debt is added, with payment later.

Do I Need to Change My Estate Plan?

Married couples often have estate plans mirroring each other. The husband's will may give all his property to the wife, and name her as personal representative, with her will doing the same. Or they may have living (*inter vivos*) trusts with each other as trustee and beneficiary. Their financial and health care powers of attorney may appoint the other spouse as agent. Spouses may also be the beneficiaries of life insurance and retirement benefits.

Even without an estate plan, spouses are entitled, by law, to many estate rights. These include the right to a share of a spouse's estate, dower (an estate that widows have in their husbands' real property), homestead (the right to live in the marital home after a spouse's death) and various allowances from the spouse's estate.

As explained in "After Your Divorce" on page 89, a divorce terminates all these estate rights. But there is always a risk that one spouse may die or become incapacitated *during* the divorce, giving the other control of the property. If you're in good health, this risk is small and not worth worrying about. But if you're in poor health, you may want to do some quick estate planning during the divorce.

There are a few things you can do yourself without a lawyer. You can revise your will or living trust naming a new personal representative in the will or a new trustee/beneficiaries in the trust. If you've appointed your spouse as agent under a financial or health care power of attorney, you can make a new one with another agent. And unless you and your spouse have agreed otherwise, you can change the designation of your spouse as beneficiary of your life insurance and retirement benefits.

To do more, you're going to need legal help. In Michigan, you normally cannot totally disinherit your spouse,* since spouses are guaranteed a minimum share of the estate. However, a lawyer can prepare a will for you reducing your spouse's share to that legal minimum. In exceptional cases, spouses can lose their estate rights by misconduct (absence, desertion, neglect for one year or more). A lawyer can tell you whether you qualify for this exception, and how to disinherit your spouse if you do.

A lawyer can also advise you about releasing estate rights. You may have already done that in a prenuptial agreement. The lawyer can tell you whether the release was effective. Michigan law doesn't normally permit the release of estate rights while a marriage is intact. But you can release them after your marriage has broken down in a postnuptial agreement. A lawyer should prepare that agreement. After any release of estate rights, you are free to benefit whomever you like in your will.

---

*   There is one way to disinherit a spouse in Michigan. You put all your property in nonprobate form for the benefit of third parties, reducing your probate estate to zero. This has the effect of disinheriting a spouse because the estate rights for spouses are satisfied from probate estates. Michigan lawmakers are considering closing this loophole by giving spouses estate rights in nonprobate property.

With a lawyer's help, you could also convert any joint tenancy property (also known as tenancy by the entirety property) into tenancy in common ownership. Unlike other forms of property, tenancy in common doesn't have rights of survivorship. So when a spouse-owner dies, the surviving spouse doesn't get everything. Instead, the deceased spouse's estate and the surviving spouse split the property. This division makes tenancy in common ideal for estranged spouses who want to keep their shares of joint property.

Do I Need "Temporary Relief"?

In most lawsuits, you normally don't get any relief (the things you're asking for in your lawsuit) unless and until you win the case. But in divorce cases it's possible to get some relief before the end of the divorce. As mentioned in "Alimony" on page 11, courts may decide alimony on a temporary basis. And as pointed out previously in this part, courts can do some temporary property division or protection during divorces.

If a court grants such temporary relief, the issue is decided until the end of the case when the court decides it finally in the divorce judgment. Temporary relief is important in contested cases, but it can be useful in uncontested ones as well. The trouble is, the legal procedures for getting temporary relief are very complicated, so this book doesn't have any instructions or forms for it.

As useful as temporary relief is, it isn't required in divorce cases, and you can often get by without it. When you are self-sufficient, you may not need any temporary alimony or property. Or if the defendant is unavailable or unable to provide any support, it may not be worth seeking.

If you believe temporary relief is necessary, you may be able to improvise a substitute. You and the defendant can arrange to have the equivalent of temporary relief provided privately out of court. For example, you and your spouse could divide property informally and/or have alimony paid without a court order, while your divorce is pending. This arrangement would resemble what you might obtain in temporary relief from the court, except that it wouldn't be legally enforceable.*

If this substitute won't work, and you believe you must have temporary relief, see a lawyer. The lawyer will prepare the necessary papers to seek the relief from the court.

Can I Socialize during the Divorce?

As couples split up, they often wonder whether they can start new social or sexual relationships. What you do during separation and divorce ought to

---

*   Another problem with paying alimony informally out of court is that the payer won't be entitled to an income tax deduction for the payments, since they're not being paid in a divorce document.

be your own business. But regrettably, extramarital activity can be interpreted as marital fault, which could hurt you.

In a contested divorce, marital fault from extramarital activity may influence property division and alimony. Marital fault usually doesn't cause problems in uncontested cases as long as everything remains agreeable. But the fault can become an issue if your agreement over the divorce falls apart.

As a result, use your common sense as you begin your single life. You don't have to live like a hermit. But you should be discreet in your new social and sexual relationships. That will prevent any possible legal trouble.

> ### More Information
>
> On adjusting to life during and after divorce:
>
> *Creative Divorce*, Mel Krantzler, New York: M. Evans and Company, Inc., 1973

Can I Keep the Divorce Secret?

Although court files are public records, courts have the power to restrict access to the contents of files by sealing them. In fact, courts once routinely sealed divorce cases between wealthy or influential people.

In 1991, new court rules were adopted governing court secrecy. Now one must file a motion to seal the file and convince the court that there is "good cause" for sealing. Because of these new rules, it's difficult to have divorce files sealed. If you want to try to get your file sealed, contact a lawyer for help.

Some local newspapers cover judicial business and publish lists of divorces granted by the courts in their area. There is really no way to keep that information out of the papers, since the completion of a divorce is a matter of public record even if the divorce file itself has been sealed.

Will I Have Tax Problems from the Divorce?

At one time, divorce was a tax nightmare. Not only were the tax rules for divorce complex, divorce itself had many negative tax consequences. These rules were changed by the Tax Reform Act of 1984 (TRA). The TRA is a rare example of a tax law that actually made the law simpler and fairer.

> ### More Information
>
> On taxes and divorce, obtain "Tax Information for Divorced or Separated Individuals" (Pub. 504) from any IRS office or call the IRS at 1-800-829-3676.

The TRA defined which divorce-related payments qualify as alimony (see "Alimony" on page 11 for more about these alimony tax rules). But the TRA doesn't alter how alimony is taxed. It's still income for the recipient and a deduction (technically an adjustment to gross income) for the payer.

The most far-reaching change wrought by the TRA is to make all transfers of property between divorcing spouses nontaxable. Previously, spouses could gain or lose income from the property divisions of their divorces. Such gain or loss from a divorce is no longer possible under the new law, although income tax problems can still crop up when a spouse sells property obtained in the divorce later.

What If My Spouse Is Mentally Incompetent?

If your spouse has been declared mentally incompetent by a probate court, s/he must be specially represented in the divorce. After a declaration of mental incompetency, the probate court may appoint a conservator (a representative like a guardian) to manage the incompetent's affairs. A conservator has the authority to represent the incompetent in a divorce.

If you have been appointed as your spouse's conservator, you won't be able to represent him/her in the divorce because of the obvious conflict of interest. But you can ask the probate court to appoint another person as conservator, and the new conservator could handle the divorce.

An alternative is to have a *guardian ad litem* (GAL) appointed for your mentally incompetent spouse. While a conservator has broad powers to manage affairs, a GAL's authority is limited to representing the incompetent in a single lawsuit. In a divorce, the court handling the divorce, not a probate court, can appoint a GAL for a spouse after the divorce is filed.

Whatever arrangements are made for your incompetent spouse, they should be completed before or soon after you file your divorce. Then you can serve the spouse's conservator or GAL with the divorce papers, and the divorce can proceed normally.

What If I Need to File a Bankruptcy?

Divorce and bankruptcy seem to go together because financial problems often cause divorce. According to one study, divorced people file for bankruptcy at three times the rate of the nondivorced population. Despite this link, divorce and bankruptcy aren't as compatible as they ought to be. Each procedure requires a separate case, filed in different court systems (divorce in state court; bankruptcy in federal court), using different laws and rules.

Because of these problems, if you're considering both a divorce and a bankruptcy, seek legal advice. The lawyer can advise you about the relationship between divorce and bankruptcy, which type of bankruptcy to file (there are several), and whether to file singly or jointly (even separated spouses are permitted to file joint bankruptcies).

Don't wait to get legal help, because the timing of a divorce and bankruptcy can be important. In some cases, it's better to file the bankruptcy before completion of the divorce to protect exempt marital property. In other cases, the divorce should be finished before the bankruptcy is started so that some debts and obligations—but never alimony—can be wiped out. There are no firm rules about the sequence of cases; the timing will depend on the nature of your property and debts. Your lawyer should be able to explain what's best in your situation.

What If I Want to Dismiss the Divorce?

According to one estimate, 20-30% of all divorces are voluntarily withdrawn and dismissed. No one knows the exact reason for all these dismissals, but it's likely that most cases were dropped after the spouses reconciled.

There's no penalty for withdrawing your divorce after you start it. On the contrary, Michigan law encourages reconciliation and dismissal throughout the divorce. That's what the statutory waiting period is for. If you and your spouse decide to reconcile, see Appendix D for instructions and forms for dismissing your divorce.

What If My Spouse Abuses Me?

The physical abuse of one spouse by the other—usually, but not always, a wife at the hands of her husband—has been a constant problem with marriage and divorce. It's been estimated that spouse abuse is a problem in one out of three marriages. Sometimes this domestic violence becomes deadly. According to recent FBI figures, nearly a third of all female homicide victims are murdered by either their husbands or boyfriends.

For years, the legal system offered abused spouses little protection. It often seemed that family violence was a private matter into which the legal system wouldn't intervene. But that attitude has changed, and Michigan's spouse abuse laws have been toughened recently. Today it's possible to get personal protection orders (PPOs) preventing your spouse from:

- assaulting, attacking, beating, wounding or molesting you or someone else
- threatening to kill or physically injure you or someone else
- stalking you or someone else
- any act or conduct interfering with personal liberty or causing a reasonable apprehension of violence
- interfering with your place of employment or jeopardizing your employment
- purchasing or possessing a firearm
- entering property (so that your spouse can be ordered away from your home, even when it's the joint marital home)
- interfering with your removal of personal property or children from your spouse's property
- removing minor children from the person with legal custody, except as allowed by a court order

You don't have to wait until a divorce to get a PPO. They're available anytime there's domestic abuse, even before you file. After filing, you can get a PPO while the divorce is pending. It's also possible to get a permanent PPO at the end of the divorce, which can remain in effect for any specified period of time.

More Information

About spouse abuse, get:

Getting Free: A Handbook for Women in Abusive Relationships, Ginny NiCarthy, Seattle: The Seal Press, 1986

On Michigan's spouse abuse laws, ask your state senator or representative for *Survivor's Handbook for Battered Women.*

To find a spouse abuse shelter in your area, call Michigan's 24-hour spouse abuse crisis line at 1-800-996-6226.

When a spouse violates a PPO, s/he can be immediately arrested by the police, even if they didn't see the violation. Violation of a PPO is both a civil and criminal contempt of court, punishable by a maximum fine of $500 and 93 days in jail.

For all the protection it offers, Michigan's PPO law is complicated, making it difficult for nonlawyers to use. That's why it's best to have a lawyer when you're facing spouse abuse. If you have a low income, you may be able to get help from legal aid. The legal aid offices are very busy, but they usually give priority to spouse abuse cases. Or you can rely on a private lawyer for help. If you're determined to represent yourself, you can obtain PPO forms and directions from the clerk of your circuit or family court. Since 1994, all Michigan circuit and family courts must make these materials available.

Whatever you do, keep in mind that a PPO cannot guarantee your safety. A court order is only a piece of paper; it will not stop someone bent on violence. If you believe your spouse is determined to harm you, take whatever precautions are necessary to protect yourself—with or without a PPO. This may even mean moving to a safe place. You may be able to find refuge with a friend or relative. There are also special shelters for abused spouses (and their children). Michigan has about 45 shelters serving every part of the state.

Can a Noncitizen Divorce in Michigan?

In the United States, divorce jurisdiction is based on residency. If you reside here you can get a divorce, regardless of your nationality. But in other countries, particularly those in civil law areas (basically the non-English-speaking world), divorce jurisdiction is determined by nationality, not residency. In these countries, you must be a citizen to get a divorce. A few countries don't bother with divorce jurisdiction at all, because they refuse to permit divorce.

If you're a citizen of one of those countries, a divorce you get in Michigan might not be recognized in your country. This won't be a problem if you've broken all ties with the country. But it could spell trouble if you intend to return to the country or have property there. To find out how a Michigan divorce will be treated in your native country, check with your embassy or consulate.

Do You Need Legal Help?

If your divorce looks too complicated for you to do yourself, you need legal help. How do you find a good lawyer? The best way is by recommendation from someone you trust. But if you can't find a lawyer by word-of-mouth, legal services and referrals are available from:

Legal aid. Those who meet federal poverty guidelines are eligible for legal aid from the 13 regional legal aid organizations located throughout the state. The problem is, these programs are often so understaffed that they can help only a fraction of those eligible for their services. To find the legal aid office in your area, look under "Legal Aid" or "Social Service Organizations" in the yellow pages.

Legal clinics and services. Newspapers often carry advertisements for low-cost uncontested divorce services. Some of these services are offered by local attorneys doing business as clinics, while others may be branches of national legal service companies.

Lawyers. These days lawyers aren't shy about advertising, and you can find their ads in newspapers and the yellow pages. County bar associations in several of the larger counties provide lawyer referral services. To obtain lawyer referrals in other counties, call the state bar referral service at 1-800-292-7850.

On the other hand, you may have decided that your divorce isn't too complicated. If that's true, you're ready to move on to Chapter 2 and begin your divorce.

Chapter 2

Preparing to Start Your Divorce

Overview of Divorce Procedure

Doing Your Divorce

After Your Divorce

Preparing to Start Your Divorce

For lawyers, an uncontested divorce isn't much more than a clerical task, which they usually assign to their secretaries. But nonlawyers are often stumped by the simplest things: How do I fill out the divorce papers? Where do I file them? When do I file them? How do I find the right court? This section deals with all these problems and more, so you will be as well-prepared as any lawyer.

Preparing Your Papers

Many divorce-filers are surprised to find that the courts won't do the divorce paperwork for you. Instead, it's your responsibility to prepare all the divorce papers. Don't try to do this all at once; prepare the papers as you need them, during each step of your divorce. If possible, you should type the papers. But if you can't, it's permissible to print them by hand in ink. Either way, make sure that the papers are neat and legible.

Your divorce papers must also be accurate and honest. Judges can penalize those who intentionally or even carelessly file false legal papers. Ordinarily, these penalties are payments of money to opponents hurt by the false papers. But for some false papers the penalties are severe. When you sign an affidavit, you swear to the notary public that the contents are true. You do much the same when you sign papers with a verification declaration ("I declare that the statements above are true to the best of my information, knowledge, and belief"). According to Michigan law, it's a crime to knowingly file a false affidavit, while the intentional falsification of a verified document is a contempt of court. Don't be alarmed by these penalties; just make sure that your papers are accurate and honest.

More Information

An affidavit is a legal paper stating facts that must be sworn to under oath before someone, such as a notary public, who can give oaths.

To obtain notary services, look in the yellow pages under "Notaries," or contact insurance agencies, banks or mailing/shipping stores.

Among your divorce papers are several forms issued by the State Court Administrative Office (SCAO). These state forms include Michigan court forms and friend of the court forms, which are coded in the lower left corner by type (MC or FOC), number and date of release. Besides these state forms, a few counties, notably Wayne (code: number/date), have local forms. Added to the state forms are several Grand River Press forms (code: GRP/number/date). The Grand River Press forms include most of the important divorce papers, such as the complaint, default and judgment. The state used to provide these forms, but discontinued them in 1989. The Grand River Press forms have been created to replace them.

Every form has a special purpose and each is prepared differently. Yet all the forms share similar captions which are filled in as follows:

| | Original - Court | 2nd copy - Defendant |
| | 1st copy - Friend of the Court | 3rd copy - Plaintiff |

STATE OF MICHIGAN JUDICIAL CIRCUIT - FAMILY DIVISION OJIBWAY COUNTY	JUDGMENT OF DIVORCE Page 1 of pages	CASE NO. 89-00501—DO JUDGE TUBBS

Court address — 200 N. MAIN, LAKE CITY, MI 48800 — Court telephone no. 773-0000

Plaintiff's name, address and social security no. DARLENE A. LOVELACE 121 S. MAIN LAKE CITY, MI 48800 PH: 772-0000 380-16-1010	V	Defendant's name, address and social security no. DUDLEY A. LOVELACE 900 S. MAPLE LAKE CITY, MI 48800 379-10-5567
Plaintiff's attorney, bar no., address and telephone no. IN PRO PER		Defendant's attorney, bar no., address and telephone no.

| | Original - Court | 2nd copy - Defendant |
| | 1st copy - Friend of the Court | 3rd copy - Plaintiff |

STATE OF MICHIGAN JUDICIAL CIRCUIT - FAMILY DIVISION OJIBWAY COUNTY	JUDGMENT OF DIVORCE Final of pages	CASE NO. 89-00501—DO

Plaintiff DARLENE A. LOVELACE	V	Defendant DUDLEY E. LOVELACE

As you can see, the papers have either a long or short caption. In a long caption, you must put the county where the divorce is filed in the upper left corner. Get the court's address and telephone number from the telephone book and place this information on the line below. In the boxes below that, insert your and your spouse's names, addresses, telephone and social security numbers. In the plaintiff's attorney box, write "In Pro Per." That phrase is an abbreviation of *in propria persona* ("in your own person"), and it says that you are doing the divorce yourself without a lawyer.

Your case number goes in the upper right corner. This number starts with a two-digit number for the year followed by several other numbers. It ends with a two-letter case-type code. All cases in Michigan have codes according to their type: A divorce with minor children bears a DM code and divorces without minor children have a DO code. Be-cause a case number isn't assigned until filing, you won't have it for your initial divorce papers, so leave the case number spaces blank on them. But include your case number in the captions of your other papers.

If you're in a larger county that has more than one circuit court judge, write the name of your judge beneath the case numbers on all the papers you file after the initial divorce papers. This will help direct the papers to the correct court file and judge.

With a short caption, you can omit much of the above information. All you need for a short caption is the court, your case number, your and your spouse's names, and the name of your judge if you're in a multi-judge circuit.

In 1987, Wayne County, which has the state's largest court system, adopted a caption labeling system to reduce the misfiling of court papers. When you file a divorce in Wayne County, the clerk prints strips of cap-tion labels for you and the defendant. Notice how the clerk takes several of these labels and affixes them to the captions of your initial divorce papers. As you file your subsequent papers, use labels from your strip to label them in the same way. Save the other strip of caption labels because you must have it served on the defen-dant later.

In Wayne County, you're required to put labels only on the captions of your original court-filed divorce papers, not the photocopies. But you can photocopy the papers after you have attached the caption labels. This should leave you with enough labels for all your divorce papers. If you run out, you can get more by writing to the Wayne County Clerk, Labels Division, 211 City-County Building, Detroit, MI 48226.

As you prepare divorce papers, you must make several photocopies. Except for the Summons and Complaint (MC 01), make two photocopies of each divorce paper. This gives you enough divorce papers and copies to distribute as follows:

- original - court (clerk)
- 1st copy - defendant
- 2nd copy - plaintiff

When you photocopy your divorce papers, make sure that you copy both sides of any two-sided forms because some papers have important information on their reverse sides. All these two-sided forms are tumble-printed, with their reverse sides upside down. This makes it possible to read the reverse sides while the papers are fastened to a file folder by simply lifting them up. When you photocopy these two-sided forms, you might not be able to run your copies through the photocopier again to get a tumble-printed form. If so, just make the paper into a two-page form and staple the pages together.

With all those papers and copies, it's easy to become disorganized. To keep track of everything, prepare a file for all your divorce papers. Not only will this file keep you organized during the divorce, it will give you a complete record of the case afterward.

Court System

Before 1998, divorce cases were handled by the general circuit courts of Michigan. On January 1, 1998, new family courts (which are technically divisions of the circuit courts) went into operation. The family courts deal with all kinds of family-related cases, including divorce, annulment, separate maintenance, paternity, juvenile delinquency, protective (abuse/neglect or dependency) and adoption cases.

The philosophy behind the family courts is that they can specialize in family law matters, unlike the general circuit courts which deal with all kinds of civil and criminal cases. The family courts also have a "one family, one judge" policy, which attempts to bring all of a family's cases before the same judge.

Family courts may be new, but the court personnel hasn't changed. The following people have responsibility for your divorce case:

Judge. Your divorce is handled by a family court judge, who is either a circuit court or probate court judge assigned to the family court. You cannot choose the judge for your case. Ordinarily, when you file the clerk randomly assigns a judge to your case. But if you or members of your family have other family law cases pending in the court, the clerk will try to assign your divorce to the judge hearing the other case(s). With this assignment, the same judge will handle all the family's cases. If you dislike the judge, you cannot get another unless you can prove that the judge is actually biased or prejudiced against you.

Clerk. The family court clerk receives all your divorce papers and maintains a court file for them. Throughout this book the family court clerk is simply called the clerk.

Courtroom clerk. The courtroom clerk sits in the courtroom next to the judge while the court is in session. During a trial, the courtroom clerk is responsible for marking and receiving exhibits offered into evidence. In an uncontested divorce case, the courtroom clerk has a smaller role, but in some counties s/he may receive and file papers during the final hearing.

Assignment clerk. Some of the larger counties use special assignment clerks to schedule court hearings. In these counties, final hearings in uncontested divorce cases may be scheduled through the assignment clerk.

Court reporter. The court reporter sits below the judge and records the court proceedings. In an uncontested divorce case, the court reporter makes a record of the final hearing, although it's unlikely that a transcript of the hearing will ever be needed.

Judge's secretary. Working in the judge's office, the judge's secretary may help in submitting papers to the judge for review.

Law clerk. Most judges have law clerks, who are often law students or recent law school graduates. Law clerks help judges with a number of tasks, including review of papers.

In many counties, these court personnel are conveniently located under one roof, usually in a courthouse or county building. But in other counties, whose court systems have outgrown their courthouses, court personnel may be scattered among several buildings. Before you begin your divorce, make sure you know where the court personnel are located.

The first person you want to find is the clerk because you will begin your divorce in the clerk's office. County clerks are officially the clerks of the family courts. In most counties, the county clerks do this clerking. But some counties assign the clerking to special family court clerks, separate from county clerks. To find out the situation in your county, call the county clerk, or look up the county government listing in the telephone book and see if there is a separate listing for a clerk of the family division of the circuit court.

Regardless of who serves as the clerk, s/he will open a court file for your case when you file your divorce. As you file papers in the case, the clerk will ordinarily use the following procedure:

- keep the original for the court file
- return a true copy* for the defendant
- return a true copy for the plaintiff

If it's inconvenient to file your papers in person, you may file by mail. You should file your initial divorce papers in person, but filing other papers by mail is easy. Just send the papers to the clerk along with a cover letter or note asking for filing and return of the copies you have enclosed. For return of the copies, include a self-addressed envelope with postage.

---

* When a clerk returns a copy of a paper to you, it may have a stamp or notation indicating that it's a true copy. A true copy is a semi-official copy of a court paper. It's not absolutely necessary to obtain true copies of your papers, but it's a good idea to get them when you can.

At the end of the divorce, you must appear in court during a final hearing and give some brief testimony. The final hearing is held in the courthouse of the judge assigned to your case. When you go to the courthouse for the hearing, arrive early so you can find the right courtroom. By arriving early, you can also take care of any last-minute details for the hearing. And if other cases are being heard before yours, you can watch and see how they are handled. This will give you tips on what you must do during your hearing.

In exceptional cases, it's permissible to give final hearing testimony by telephone or other electronic means, without appearing in court. Prisoners and the physically handicapped may be able to qualify for this exception.

Paying Fees

You must pay several fees to get a divorce (see "How Much Will My Divorce Cost?" on page 28 for a description of the fees). Except for the service fee, you pay these fees to the clerk. Clerks usually accept cash, personal checks or money orders as payment. After you pay, the clerk may give you a receipt, which you should keep as proof of payment.

The service fee is paid outside of court. As mentioned before, you can choose from among several methods of service: 1) acknowledgment 2) mail 3) delivery. You can usually obtain service by acknowledgment for free. When you use service by mail, you pay the post office for the mailing. If you use service by delivery, you pay the server, who is usually a sheriff or commercial process server. Ordinarily, the server bills you for the service fee after service when s/he returns the proof of service to you. But if you use service by delivery out of town or out of state, it's a good idea to prepay the service fee. When you send the service papers to the server, include a check or money order for $25 or so, and a note asking the server to refund/bill you for the difference between his service fee and your prepayment.

If you qualify, you can get an exemption from payment of the court fees. Appendix A explains how to obtain a fee exemption by using the Affidavit and Order, Suspension of Fees/Costs (MC 20). If you've received a fee exemption, you won't have to pay any court fees during your divorce (although you might have to pay them at the end of the divorce). If the clerk tries to charge you a fee during your divorce, refer the clerk to the Affidavit and Order, Suspension of Fees/Costs (MC 20), which will be in your court file.

Figuring Time

During your divorce, you must deal with several important time periods, including: 1) 180-day state residency requirement 2) 10-day county residency requirement 3) answering period (usually 21 or 28 days) 4) statutory waiting period (60 days for divorces without minor children) 5) filing deadlines for various papers.

The court rules have detailed provisions to figure these periods of time. For a time period of days, the period begins on the day after the day of an act (filing, service, establishment of residency, etc.). The day of the act itself isn't counted. The last day of the period is counted, unless it falls on a Saturday, Sunday or legal holiday. In that case, the period extends to the next day that isn't a Saturday, Sunday or legal holiday.

> *Example:* You serve a defendant by mail on May 1. The 28-day answering period after service by mail begins on May 2 (the day after the day of service) and ends on May 29 (which in this example is not a Saturday, Sunday or legal holiday). The defendant would then have until May 29 to answer.

> *Example:* You serve a defendant by mail on May 1. The 28-day answering period after service by mail begins on May 2 (the day after the day of service) and ends on May 29. But this year May 29 is Memorial Day, a legal holiday, so the answering period extends to May 30. The defendant then must answer by May 30.

If all this seems too complicated, the easiest thing to do is estimate the time period and then add some more time, as a cushion, to be safe. For example, if you figure that a time period ends sometime during the first week of a month, you could wait until the middle of the month to take action. It's permissible to estimate time like this because you don't have to rush things in an uncontested divorce.

Local Rules and Forms

For years, there were variations in divorce procedures among Michigan's 83 counties. In 1993, the state tried to standardize procedures by abolishing all local divorce rules and forms. But later, several counties, including Wayne, were permitted to readopt some of their old rules and forms. In the future, other local rules and forms may creep back into use.

So don't panic if you encounter some local practices that aren't described in this book. Ask the local authorities what the local practice is and adapt to it. Luckily, variations tend to be minor. They typically concern scheduling the final hearing.

New Laws, Rules, Forms and Fees

These days, divorce laws, rules, forms and fees change regularly. Congress and the Michigan Legislature are constantly passing new divorce laws. Added to this are the thousands of decisions courts issue each year, some of which affect divorce.

As a result of this activity, parts of this book may become outdated. To keep the book current, Grand River Press offers an update about recent changes in divorce law. See the order form in the front of this book for update information.

Overview of Divorce Procedure

At first, divorce procedure may seem forbidding. But it's really not so mysterious when you break it down into steps and understand the purpose of each step.

Like any lawsuit, a divorce starts when the plaintiff files a paper known as a complaint. Despite its rather alarming name, a complaint is simply the document that starts a lawsuit. After filing, the clerk issues a summons in the case. These papers (and possibly another) make up the initial divorce papers.

The defendant must get notice of the divorce by receiving the initial divorce papers. Notice is provided by serving these papers on the defendant. There are three regular methods of service, plus a couple of alternate methods for elusive or disappeared defendants.

After service, the defendant may respond to the plaintiff's complaint within an answering period. The defendant's response can be either by filing: 1) an answer to the complaint or 2) a motion objecting to the complaint.

In the vast majority of cases, defendants don't bother to respond, putting them in default. The plaintiff can then go to the clerk and have the defendant's default declared. With the default, the case is officially an uncontested divorce, or what lawyers sometimes call a *pro confesso* or "pro con" divorce case.

But if the defendant responds to the complaint within the answering period, the divorce is contested. In that case, the plaintiff should seek a lawyer to take over the case because it's extremely difficult to handle a contested case without a lawyer.

After the 60-day statutory waiting period, the plaintiff can get the divorce judgment during the final hearing. The plaintiff must appear at the hearing and give testimony or "proofs" in support of the judgment. This sounds scary, but the final hearing is usually very brief and easy to get through. After the final hearing, the plaintiff files the divorce judgment making the divorce final.

This book has organized the divorce procedure into four steps: "Filing," "Service," "Default" and "Final Hearing." The flowchart below summarizes these steps and the time to perform them.

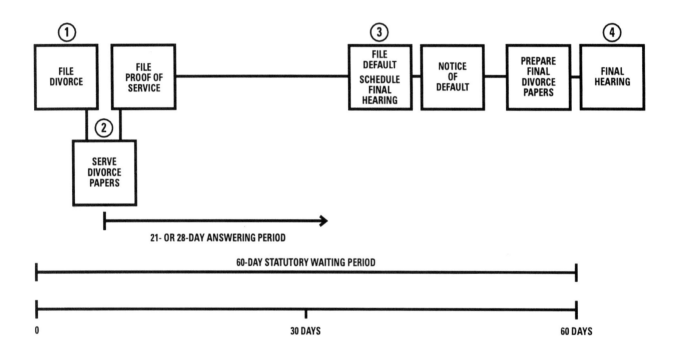

1 Filing

You begin your divorce by preparing the initial divorce papers. These papers include the complaint and summons. The divorce complaint describes the basic facts of your marriage. It also tells the court that your marriage has broken down by citing the no-fault grounds for divorce. Finally, the complaint asks the court to decide the divorce issues. The purpose of the summons is to notify the defendant that you have filed a divorce complaint, and that s/he may respond to it.

The complaint and summons are contained in a set of forms: the Summons and Complaint (MC 01) and Complaint for Divorce (GRP 1). The Summons and Complaint (MC 01) includes the summons in the case along with the first part of the complaint. The Complaint for Divorce (GRP 1) is actually a continuation of this form and contains the remainder of the complaint.

Your initial divorce papers will include the Affidavit and Order, Suspension of Fees/Costs (MC 20) when you want a fee exemption (see Appendix A for the form and instructions). You must file an extra paper and take other special steps if you seek alimony (see Appendix C for the details).

If you have a prenuptial agreement that you want to use for property division, you must include it among your initial divorce papers. The court rules say that anytime a contract is part of a lawsuit a copy of the contract must be attached to the complaint as an exhibit. Since a prenuptial agreement is a type of contract, a copy of it must be attached to your Complaint for Divorce (GRP 1) as an exhibit.

After paragraph #7 of the complaint, add the phrase: "according to a prenuptial agreement attached as Exhibit A." Make several photocopies of the prenuptial agreement and write "Exhibit A" at the top of the front page of each copy. Attach these copies to the complaint and all copies of the complaint.

The blank forms for the initial divorce papers and all the other divorce papers are located in the forms section in the back of this book. Special forms (like the Affidavit and Order, Suspension of Fees/Costs (MC 20)) and local forms (like the Certificate of Conformity for Domestic Relations Order or Judgment (1225) for Wayne County divorces) are located in a special section. All the forms are perforated so you can easily tear them out of the book.

( ) = optional practice

[ ] = local practice

There are filled-in samples of the initial divorce papers at the end of this section. Sample forms also appear at the ends of other sections and appendices. For general information about form preparation, see "Preparing Your Papers" on page 45.

Ordinarily, you must make two photocopies of your divorce papers. The clerk gets the original, leaving copies for the defendant and you. But you will need an extra copy of the Summons and Complaint (MC 01), giving you the following papers:

•	Summons and Complaint	MC 01	3
•	Complaint for Divorce	GRP 1	2
(•	Affidavit and Order, Suspension of Fees/Costs	MC 20	2)

Filing Your Divorce

Start your divorce by filing it with the clerk (see "Court System" on page 48 for information about finding the clerk). To file, you must have your initial divorce papers ready. And unless you receive a fee exemption, you must pay the filing fee (see "How Much Will My Divorce Cost?" on page 28 for the amount of the filing fee). In all, you should have the following items when you go to the clerk's office to file your divorce:

•	Summons and Complaint	MC 01
	• original	
	• 3 copies	
•	Complaint for Divorce	GRP 1
	• original	
	• 2 copies	
•	money for the filing fee	
(•	Affidavit and Order, Suspension of Fees/Costs	MC 20)
	• original	
	• 2 copies	

When you arrive at the clerk's office, tell the clerk that you want to file a divorce complaint. The clerk should then do the following to file your divorce:

■ Take the Summons and Complaint (MC 01) and the three copies and: 1) assign a judge to the case and stamp his/her name on these papers 2) enter a case number on them 3) complete the summons boxes in the middle of the papers. File the Summons and Complaint (MC 01) and return three copies to you.

■ File the Complaint for Divorce (GRP 1) and return two copies to you.

■ Take the money for the filing fee

(■ File the Affidavit and Order, Suspension of Fees/Costs (MC 20), if used, to suspend the fees immediately; or submit the form to the judge for consideration. Return two copies to you.)

[■ In Wayne County only, prepare caption labels, label the captions of the initial divorce papers and give you two strips of caption labels.]

Before you leave the clerk's office, ask for a Record of Divorce or Annulment (B 42). This form asks for personal and marital information. You complete and file it at the end of the divorce, when you get the judgment. After filing, the clerk sends the Record of Divorce or Annulment (B 42) to the Michigan Department of Public Health for addition to the state's vital records. Although you won't use the Record of Divorce or Annulment (B 42) until later, it's convenient to pick it up now while you're at the clerk's office.

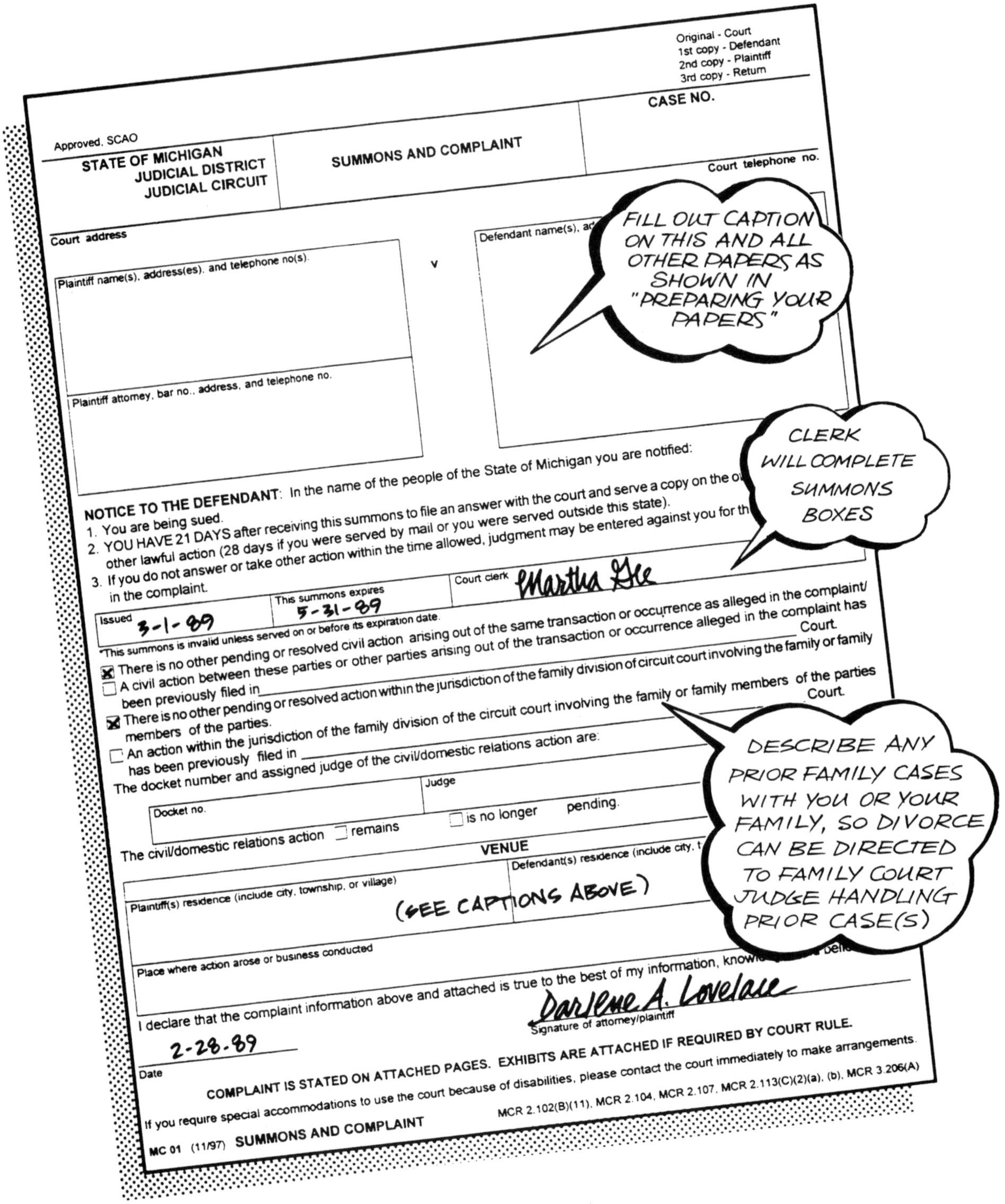

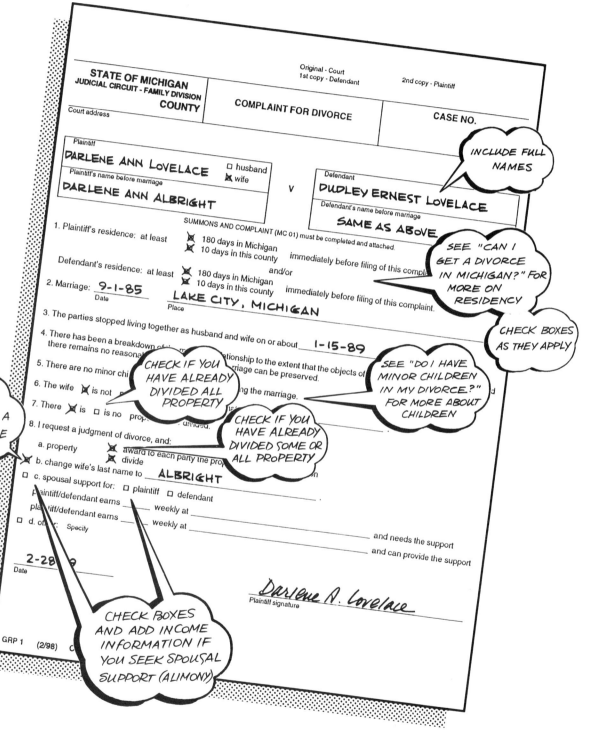

2 Service

Naturally, the defendant is entitled to notice of the divorce since s/he must have an opportunity to respond to it. Notice is provided by serving copies of the initial divorce papers on the defendant. You should begin service as soon as possible, within a few days after filing.

Although the purpose of service is notice, don't assume that you can skip it when the defendant already knows about the divorce. And don't try to serve the defendant by simply giving the divorce papers to him/her. No doubt your spouse would get informal notice of the divorce these ways. But the law requires that the defendant receive *official* notice of the divorce by service.

Official notice can only be accomplished by one of the service methods described below. With one of these methods, the court knows for sure that the defendant got notice of the divorce. For this reason, service is absolutely necessary. The service rules may seem artificial and even rather silly at times, but they must be followed carefully. If you omit service, or violate the service rules, there's a chance your whole divorce will be invalid.

There are three methods of serving defendants who are available to be served: 1) acknowledgment 2) mail 3) delivery. Each method can be used anywhere in the state of Michigan. These service methods can also be used outside the state (including foreign countries), as long as there is Michigan jurisdiction over the nonresident defendant (see "Can I Get a Divorce in Michigan?" on page 24 for more about jurisdiction).

Despite service's wide reach, there are a few minor restrictions on serving papers. The court rules disqualify you from serving the initial divorce papers personally because you're a party to the case. Instead, you must have a neutral third party serve the papers for you. If you use service by delivery, a professional server, such as a sheriff or commercial process server, can serve for you. But when you choose either service by acknowledgment or service by mail, you must enlist a helper,* such as a friend, to

---

*   The helper can be any mentally competent adult (person over 18 years of age).

help with service. The helper acts as a straw man through whose hands the divorce papers pass to the defendant.

Whatever service method you choose, you mustn't have the divorce papers served on a Sunday, an election day, or on the defendant while s/he is at, en route or returning from a court appearance. Michigan law gives people immunity from service in all these situations.

Preparing for Service

The defendant must be served with the service papers. These include the following items:

- Summons and Complaint   MC 01

- Complaint for Divorce   GRP 1

(• Affidavit and Order, Suspension of Fees/Costs   MC 20)

[• a strip of caption labels (in Wayne County only)]

After the defendant is served with these papers, service must be proved in a proof of service. Each method of service (acknowledgment, mail, deliver) is proved differently. But all are proved in the Proof of Service on the reverse of your extra copy of the Summons and Complaint (MC 01). This paper is called the "proof of service copy of the Summons and Complaint (MC 01)." After service, you file it with the clerk so that your court file shows that the defendant was served.

Service by Acknowledgment

Service by acknowledgment is the simplest method of service. To use this method, you need the cooperation of the defendant and the assistance of a helper. If the defendant is in another county or state, you must find someone to act as the helper there. Service is accomplished by having the helper hand the service papers to the defendant. You may be present during the transfer but the helper, not you, must be the one who actually hands the service papers to the defendant. The day of service is the day the defendant receives the service papers from the helper.

Proving Service by Acknowledgment

Immediately after service, the helper should have the defendant date (with time and day) and sign the Acknowledgment of Service, which is at the bottom of the reverse of your proof of service copy of the Summons and Complaint (MC 01). Make two copies of this paper and save for filing later as your proof of service.

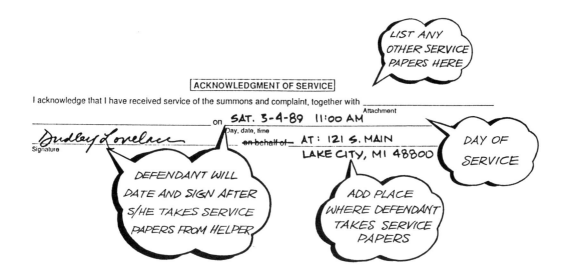

Service by Mail

Service by mail is a little more expensive than service by acknowledgment. But it's a very effective method of service because it goes anywhere U.S. mail is delivered—even overseas.* The court rules permit service by mail through either registered or certified mail. Because certified mail is cheaper than registered mail, you will probably want to choose certified mail.

When you serve by mail, you need the assistance of a helper and the U.S. Postal Service. Your helper mails the service papers to the defendant and the postal service delivers these to him/her by certified mail.

To prove service, you need several special services available with certified mail: 1) restricted delivery 2) return receipt service showing the person receiving the papers and the date and address of delivery. By restricting delivery, the service papers are delivered only to the defendant personally or someone s/he has designated in writing to receive mail. The return receipt provides proof of who received the papers and the date and address of delivery. This receipt is a key part of the proof of service.

Before you have the service papers mailed, prepare the mailing by placing your service papers in an envelope addressed to the defendant with your helper's name and address as the return address. In addition, you or your helper must prepare two certified mail forms: 1) Receipt for Certified Mail (PS Form 3800) 2) Domestic Return Receipt (PS Form 3811), which are available at any post office. Your helper's name and address should go on the front of the Domestic Return Receipt (PS Form 3811). The reverse of that

---

*   The service by mail described above deals with mail sent inside the United States. For service by mail in foreign countries, ask the post office about recorded delivery, which is similar to domestic certified mail.

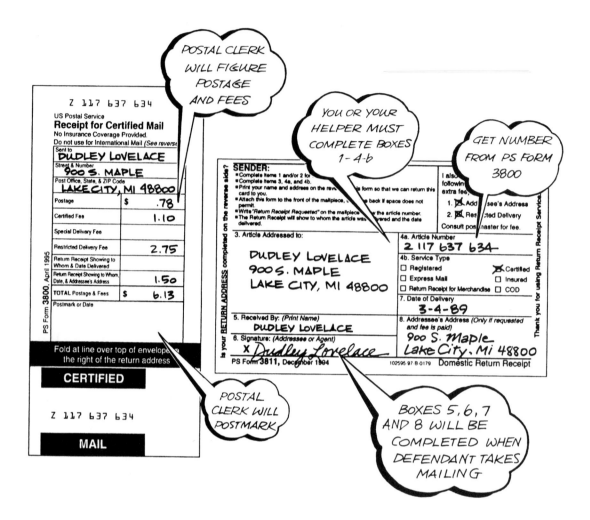

form and the Receipt for Certified Mail (PS Form 3800) should be completed as shown above.

Have your helper take the envelope containing the service papers, the certified mail forms (PS Form 3800 and PS Form 3811) and money to pay for the mailing to a post office window. The helper should ask the postal clerk to mail the envelope by certified mail with the special services you have checked on the Domestic Return Receipt (PS Form 3811). The clerk will prepare the certified mailing and return a postmarked Receipt for Certified Mail (PS Form 3800) to your helper. Keep this receipt for your records.

Later, a letter carrier will deliver the mailing to the defendant, get his/her signature in box #5 on the Domestic Return Receipt (PS Form 3811), and complete boxes #7 and #8 on the receipt. Within a few days, your helper should get the Domestic Return Receipt (PS Form 3811) back in the mail. You can then have your helper prove the service as described below. The day of service is the day the defendant receives the mailing from the letter carrier.

If your helper gets the envelope back, instead of the Domestic Return Receipt (PS Form 3811), service by mail has failed. The defendant may have refused to accept the mailing, wasn't home or has moved without leaving a current forwarding order. Whatever the case, you will have to abandon service by mail because it only works when the defendant is ready and willing to take the certified mailing from the letter carrier. If service by mail fails, try service by delivery instead.

Proving Service by Mail

After your helper gets the Domestic Return Receipt (PS Form 3811) back in the mail, have him/her prove service on the reverse of your proof of service copy of the Summons and Complaint (MC 01). Complete the information about the service by mail under the Affidavit of Process Server, and have the helper sign the form before a notary public. As proof of the defendant's receipt of the mailing, staple the Domestic Return Receipt (PS Form 3811) to the reverse of your proof of service copy of the Summons and Complaint (MC 01). Make two copies of this paper and save for filing later as your proof of service.

	SUMMONS AND COMPLAINT
PROOF OF SERVICE	Case No.

TO PROCESS SERVER: You are to serve the summons and complaint not later than 91 days from the date of filing. You must make and file your return with the court clerk. If you are unable to complete service you must return this original and all copies to the court clerk.

CERTIFICATE / AFFIDAVIT OF SERVICE / NON-SERVICE

☐ OFFICER CERTIFICATE   OR   ☒ AFFIDAVIT OF PROCESS SERVER

I certify that I am a sheriff, deputy sheriff, bailiff, appointed court officer, or attorney for a party [MCR 2.104(A)(2)], and that: (notary not required)

Being first duly ... a legally competent adult who ... a corporate party, and that:

LIST ANY OTHER SERVICE PAPERS HERE

☐ I served personally a copy of the summons and complaint,
☒ I served by registered or certified mail (copy of return receipt attached) ... and complaint,

together with _____ on the defendant(s):
   Attachment

Defendant's name	Complete address(es) of service	Day, date, time
DUDLEY LOVELACE	900 S. MAPLE, LAKE CITY, MI 48800	SAT. 3-4-89

GET DATE FROM PS FORM 3811

DAY OF SERVICE

☐ After diligent search and inquiry, I have been unable to find and serve the following defendant(s):

_____

I have made the following efforts in attempting to serve process: _____

☐ I have personally attempted to serve the summons and complaint, together with _____
      Attachment

_____ on _____
                Name

at _____ and have been unable to complete service because
   Address
the address was incorrect at the time of filing.

Ruth Darling
Signature

Service fee	Miles traveled	Mileage fee	Total fee	Title
$		$	$	OJIBWAY County, Michigan.

Subscribed and sworn to before me on **3-7-89**
               Date

My commission expires: **1-1-90**   Signature: *Loretta Smiley*
         Date   Deputy court clerk/Notary public

Service by Delivery

You can also obtain service by having someone deliver the service papers to the defendant. Any mentally competent adult except you can do that. If the defendant is cooperative, you could have a helper perform service by delivery for you. But in that case it would be much easier to have the defendant simply acknowledge delivery of the service papers from your helper and get service by acknowledgment. Therefore, it's likely that you will use service by delivery for defendants who live out of town or state, or are otherwise hard to serve.

Service by delivery is usually carried out by a professional server, such as a sheriff or commercial process server. Whatever your other service options are, county sheriff departments will always serve papers for you. They often have a separate division or deputy in charge of service. In small towns or rural areas, the sheriff may be the only choice for service. But larger cities usually have commercial process servers as an alternative to the sheriff.

Both types of servers charge fees for service. By law, sheriffs charge a basic service fee of $16 plus mileage for travel to and from the defendant. However, a sheriff's service fee can be suspended if you get a fee exemption (see Appendix A for details). Even if you have to pay, sheriffs' service fees are normally cheaper than those of commercial process servers, who often charge upward of $20 for service. On the other hand, commercial process servers may be more persistent in finding and serving defendants.

Whomever you choose, you can often reduce the service fees by having the defendant pick up the service papers at the server's office. This saves the server's mileage fee. It also spares the defendant the possible embarrassment of being served with legal papers at home or work. If the defendant is willing, tell the server that the defendant will pick up the papers and then have the defendant call the server to arrange a time for the pick-up.

To obtain service by delivery in your area, take the service papers along with your proof of service copy of the Summons and Complaint (MC 01) to the server and ask for service on the defendant. The server will serve the defendant at the address in the captions of your papers. If the defendant can be found at another place, tell the server about the other address.

When the defendant lives in another county or state, you must find a server near the defendant. Call directory information for the county seat of defendant's county and get the number of the sheriff department there. Call the sheriff department and get its mailing address. If your public library has telephone books, use them to find the address of the sheriff department or a commercial process server in the defendant's county. Commercial process servers are usually listed under "Process Servers" in the yellow pages.

After you find a server, mail the service papers and your proof of service copy of the Summons and Complaint (MC 01) to the server. Enclose a note asking for service and return of a proof of service (see also "Paying Fees" on page 50 for suggestions about prepaying an out-of-town server's service fee).

When you're seeking service outside the state of Michigan, you should mention in your note that the server must prove service in the Affidavit of Process server, on the reverse of the proof of service copy of the Summons and Complaint (MC 01). An out-of-state process server must use the affidavit, instead of the Officer Certificate, because only Michigan court officers (such as Michigan sheriffs and their deputies) may use the certificate.

If all goes as planned, the server will find the defendant and deliver the service papers to him/her. The day of service is the day the server delivers the service papers to the defendant.

Proving Service by Delivery

After service, the server will prove service on the reverse of the proof of service copy of the Summons and Complaint (MC 01) that you gave the server. For service by Michigan court officers, the proof of service will appear in the Officer Certificate. All other servers must use the Affidavit of Process Server.

After service is proved, the server will return your proof of service copy of the Summons and Complaint (MC 01) to you. Make two copies of this paper and save for filing later as your proof of service.

	SUMMONS AND COMPLAINT

PROOF OF SERVICE

COMMERCIAL OR OUT-OF-STATE SERVERS MUST USE AFFIDAVIT

TO PROCESS SERVER: You are to serve the summons and complaint not later th... make and file your return with the court clerk. If you are unable to complete service to the court clerk.

You must ...ll copies

CERTIFICATE / AFFIDAVIT OF SERVICE / N...

☒ OFFICER CERTIFICATE	OR	☐ AFFIDAVIT
I certify that I am a sheriff, deputy sheriff, bailiff, appointed court officer, or attorney for a party [MCR 2.104(A)(2)], and that: (notary not required)		Being first duly sworn, I state that I am a legally competent adult who is not a party or an officer of a corporate party, and that: (notary requ...)

☒ I served personally a copy of the summons and complaint,
☐ I served by registered or certified mail (copy of return receipt attached)

LIST ANY OTHER SERVICE PAPERS HERE and complaint,

together with _____ the defendant(s):
　　　　　　　Attachment

Defendant's name	Complete address(es) of service	Day, date, time
DUDLEY LOVELACE	200 N. MAIN, LAKE CITY, MI 48800	SAT. 3-4-89 11:00 AM

SERVER WILL COMPLETE THESE BOXES

DAY OF SERVICE

☐ After diligent search and inquiry, I have ...   following defend...

I have made the following efforts in attempting to serve process: _____

☐ I have personally attempted to serve the summons and complaint, together with _____
　　　　　　　　　　　　　　　　　　　　　　　　　　　　　　　　Attachment

_____ on _____
　　　　　　　　　　　　　Name

at _____ and have been unable to complete service because
　　Address

the address was incorrect at the time of filing.

Chester Gunn
Signature
DEPUTY SHERIFF
Title

Service fee	Miles traveled	Mileage fee	Total fee
$ 10.00		$	$ 10.00

Subscribed and sworn to before me on _____ , _____ County, Michigan.
　　　　　　　　　　　　　　　　　Date

My commission expires: _____   Signature: _____
　　　　　　　　　　Date　　　　　　　　　　　　　Deputy court clerk/Notary public

Using Alternate Service

The three methods of service described above work only if the defendant is available for service. But if the defendant is elusive or has disappeared, you must resort to some form of alternate service. Appendix B has complete instructions and forms for serving elusive or disappeared defendants.

If you're convinced you need alternate service, don't wait too long to seek it. The summons in the Summons and Complaint (MC 01) lasts for 91 days after it's issued (this expiration date should have been inserted by the clerk on the front of the summons). If you fail to complete service within that time, the summons will expire and the clerk will dismiss your case (see below for more on the danger of dismissal).

There is a way to ask the judge for a new summons before the old one expires, but it's a lot of bother. The better way is to use alternate service as soon as it becomes apparent that regular service methods aren't working.

Filing the Proof of Service

Whatever method of service you use, be sure to file the proof of service soon after service is completed. This is important because delay in filing the proof of service can result in dismissal of your divorce.

As mentioned above, a summons expires after 91 days. When there's no proof of service on file after 91 days, the clerk will assume that service has failed and begin dismissal of the case for "no progress." (The clerk should give advance warning of dismissal by sending you a Notice of Intent to Dismiss (MC26).) After dismissal for no progress, you can file a motion asking the judge to reinstate the case. But reinstatement is not guaranteed, and the judge may deny the motion. In that case, you would have to refile your divorce and start over.

Divorces without minor children are usually finished before the summons expires. But sometimes there can be unexpected delays. To avoid the risk of dismissal, make sure that you file the proof of service quickly, well before the 91-day summons expiration period elapses. Take/send the proof of service, which is on the reverse of your proof of service copy of the Summons and Complaint (MC 01),* plus two copies to the clerk. The clerk will file the original and return two copies to you.

---

* If alternate service was used, the proof of service is on the reverse of either the MC 304 or MC 307.

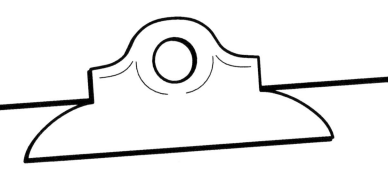

1 Filing

Filed with the clerk during filing:

□ Summons and Complaint   MC 01 / GRP 1

□ Complaint for Divorce

(□ Affidavit and Order, Suspension of Fees/Costs MC 20)

Requested from clerk during filing (for use later):

□ Record of Divorce or Annulment   B 42

[□ two strips of caption labels (in Wayne County only)]

2 Service

Service papers served on the defendant:

□ Summons and Complaint   MC 01 / GRP 1

□ Complaint for Divorce

[□ a strip of caption labels (in Wayne County only)]

(□ Affidavit and Order, Suspension of Fees/Costs MC 20)

Filed with the clerk soon after service:

□ proof of service   MC 01

3 Default

You've filed the divorce and given notice of it by service. After several weeks, you're ready for the final part of your divorce, which begins with the default.

Getting a default is important because it means that the defendant isn't contesting the divorce. Until then, you're relying on the defendant's word that the divorce is agreeable. But with the default, your divorce becomes *officially* uncontested, making it impossible for the defendant to re-enter and contest the case without special permission from the court.

Although you may be anxious to get the default, you must wait and see if the defendant responds to your divorce complaint. S/he can respond by filing with the court and sending you either: 1) an Answer to your complaint 2) a motion objecting to the complaint. If the defendant does neither, you can go ahead and apply for a default from the clerk.

To avoid default, the defendant must respond in one of those two ways within the applicable answering period. All answering periods begin the day after the day of service (see "Figuring Time" on page 50 for more on computing time periods). But the length of answering periods depends on the manner of service. The chart on the next page depicts this.

Your copy of the proof of service, which you should have filed earlier, shows the day of service. Use that and the chart to figure the answering period in your case. If the defendant hasn't responded by the end of that answering period, you're ready to get the default.

Although your divorce may only be several weeks old when you apply for the default, it's not too early to schedule the final hearing for your case. As mentioned before, Michigan law requires you to appear in court at a final hearing to receive your divorce judgment. Final hearings in divorce cases are usually heard on special days, called motion days, that courts set aside each week or month. During these motion days, judges may hear many final hearings, often at 10- or 15-minute intervals. Nevertheless, judges' motion day schedules fill up quickly, so it's a good idea to schedule your final

Answering Periods

Method of service	Day of service	Answering period
Service by acknowledgment	Day defendant takes the service papers from helper	21 days in Michigan or 28 days out of state
Service by mail	Day defendant takes the mailing of the service papers from letter carrier	28 days
Service by delivery	Day server delivers the service papers to defendant	21 days in Michigan or 28 days out of state
Alternate service		
Mailing	Day the service papers are sent	28 days
Tacking	Day the service papers are tacked to door	28 days
Household delivery	Day the service papers are delivered to person in defendant's household	28 days
Publication	Day of final publication of advertisement	Set by judge in MC 307 (a minimum of 28 days after final publication date)
Posting	Last day of posting period	Set by judge in MC 307 (a minimum of 28 days after last day of posting period)

hearing at the time of the default. If you wait, you risk delaying the conclusion of your divorce.

As previously mentioned, Michigan has imposed a 60-day waiting period on divorce cases without minor children (see "How Long Will My Divorce Take?" on page 27 for more on statutory waiting periods). This means that at least 60 days must elapse between the day you filed your divorce (this date is stamped on your Summons and Complaint (MC 01)) and the day of your final hearing.

Although you may want to get your divorce over with sooner, you must observe the waiting period. So when you schedule your final hearing, set it for a day at least 60 days after the day you filed your divorce (see "Figuring Time" on page 50 for more about figuring time in days).

Courts use several methods to schedule final hearings in uncontested divorce cases. In many counties, you can schedule a final hearing orally. When you get the default, ask the clerk to schedule a final hearing sometime after the statutory waiting period has expired. The clerk will reserve a time for you on the schedule or calendar on an appropriate motion day (make sure that you make a note of the time and date).

In other counties, you must file a written request for a final hearing. In Wayne County, for example, you must request a final hearing on a special request form known as a praecipe. Wayne County's praecipe is a yellow slip of paper called the At Issue Praecipe for Default Judgment in Domestic Relations Action, which is available from the assignment clerk in the City-County Building. You file the At Issue Praecipe for Default Judgment in Domestic Relations Action with the assignment clerk after you have gotten a default from the (county) clerk. The assignment clerk will schedule your final hearing and mail a notice of its time and date to you. Several other counties also use praecipes or similar written forms. If your county is among them, ask the clerk for the particular form and use it as directed.

In some counties, such as Oakland, the clerk will schedule the final hearing for you. These counties typically have computerized case management systems that set final hearings automatically. After the hearing is set, a notice of the time and date will be sent to you.

As you can see, there is a great deal of variation when it comes to scheduling final hearings. In fact, there is probably more variation here than in any other part of divorce procedure. To find out the practice in your county, ask the clerk when you get the default.

Getting the Default

When the defendant has failed to respond to your complaint within the applicable answering period, s/he has defaulted, allowing you to apply to the clerk for a default. The clerk declares or enters the default, but you must prepare the Default (GRP 2) form.

The Default (GRP 2) does more than simply establish the defendant's default. It also contains a nonmilitary affidavit, which is required by the federal Soldiers' and Sailors' Civil Relief Act (SSCRA). This act protects active-duty U.S. military servicepersons from lawsuits they can't respond to because of absence in the service (see "What If My Spouse or I Am in the Military Service?" on page 27 for more about the act).

The nonmilitary affidavit appears in paragraph #2 of the Default (GRP 2). It tells the court that the defendant isn't in the active-duty military service so the SSCRA doesn't apply to your case. If you've personally observed the defendant recently, you will know whether s/he is in the military service, and can truthfully say that the defendant isn't in the military.*

If the defendant has disappeared and you're using alternate service, you won't have personal knowledge about his/her (non)military status and

---

*   If you know for a fact that the defendant is in the military service, you won't be able to complete the nonmilitary affidavit. See "What If My Spouse or I Am in the Military Service?" on page 27 about why you need legal representation when the defendant is in the military.

cannot swear that the defendant isn't in the military. Luckily, there are ways to establish a person's (non)military status, allowing you to complete the nonmilitary affidavit and the divorce.

All branches of the military have worldwide locator services that can verify whether or not the defendant is a serviceperson. You can write letters to these locator services requesting information about the defendant's (non)military status.

A request form, Request for Certification of Military Status, is included in this book. You should prepare the form and make five photocopies. Send them to all five military services, with self-addressed return envelopes and any search fees.

If all goes well, you should receive certifications showing that the defendant isn't in the military services. With this information, you can then truthfully say in paragraph #2 of the Default (GRP 2) that the defendant isn't in the military service. As proof, attach the certifications to the Default (GRP 2), and photocopies to all copies of the default.

You can apply to the clerk for the default by mail or personally. Applying in person is best because you can also schedule the final hearing orally or by written request during the visit. Either way, when you apply for the default you should have:

- Default   GRP 2
    - original
    - 2 copies

[• praecipe (if needed to schedule the final hearing)]

Tell the clerk you want to file a default. The clerk should do the following:

■ Take the Default (GRP 2) and the two copies and complete the Entry section of these papers. File the original Default (GRP 2) and return two copies to you.

■ After your oral or written request (by praecipe), schedule a final hearing for your case (unless you do it elsewhere or later).

After the Default

Despite the fact that the defendant is removed from the case when you get a default, s/he is due a final notice about the default and upcoming final hearing. By giving this notice, the defendant can't complain later that s/he didn't know about the default and the divorce judgment.

After you get the default, prepare the Notice section of the Notice of Entry of Default and Request for Default Judgment of Divorce (GRP 3). Make a photocopy of the paper and attach a copy of the Default (GRP 2). Send the two papers to the defendant by ordinary first-class mail. If the defendant has disappeared, send the papers to his/her last known address.

If possible, send the Notice of Entry of Default and Request for Default Judgment of Divorce (GRP 3) with attached Default (GRP 2) to the defendant a few days after the default. But if you haven't gotten a final hearing date by then (because in some counties the court will schedule it and mail you a notice), you must wait until the final hearing is scheduled. This might be anytime during the statutory waiting period. But don't wait too long, since the court rules say that the Notice of Entry of Default and Request for Default Judgment of Divorce (GRP 3) must be sent to the defendant *no later than seven days before your final hearing.*

After you send the Notice of Entry of Default and Request for Default Judgment of Divorce (GRP 3) with attached Default (GRP 2) to the defendant, complete the Proof of Mailing section of the original Notice of Entry of Default and Request for Default Judgment of Divorce (GRP 3), and make a photocopy of the form. Then file/send the Notice of Entry of Default and Request for Default Judgment of Divorce (GRP 3) to the clerk.

Original - Court   2nd copy - Defendant
1st copy - Friend of the Court   3rd copy - Plaintiff

CASE NO.

STATE OF MICHIGAN
JUDICIAL CIRCUIT - FAMILY DIVISION
COUNTY

DEFAULT
Application, Nonmilitary Affidavit
and Entry

Court telephone no.

Court address

Plaintiff's name, address and social security no.

v

Defendant's name, address and social security no.

Plaintiff's attorney, bar no., address and telephone no.

Defendant's attorney, bar no., address and telephone no.

APPLICATION AND NONMILITARY AFFIDAVIT

INSERT DAY OF SERVICE

I request the clerk to enter the default of the defendant for failure to appear, plead or otherwise defend as provided by law.
In support of this request, I state:

1. As shown by the proof of service on file, the defendant was served with a summons and complaint on **3-4-89**,
   which is more than 21 days ago (28 days if served by mail or out of state).

2. The defendant is not an infant, incompetent person or in the military service.

Darlene A. Lovelace
Plaintiff signature

4-10-89
Date

Subscribed and sworn to before me on **4-10-89**

Loretta Smiley
Notary Public
OJIBWAY County, Michigan

My commission expires: **1-1-90**

ENTRY

CLERK WILL DATE AND SIGN

The default of the defendant is entered for failure to appear, plead or otherwise defend.

Martha Gee
Court clerk

4-11-89
Date

GRP 2   (2/98)   DEFAULT, Application, Nonmilitary Affidavit and Entry

STATE OF MICHIGAN
JUDICIAL CIRCUIT - FAMILY DIVISION
COUNTY

Court address

Original - Court
1st copy - Friend of the Court

2nd copy - Defendant
3rd copy - Plaintiff

**NOTICE OF ENTRY OF DEFAULT
AND REQUEST FOR
DEFAULT JUDGMENT OF DIVORCE**

CASE NO.

Court telephone no.

Plaintiff's name, address and social security no.

v

Defendant's name, address and social security no.

Plaintiff's attorney, bar no., address and telephone no.

Defendant's attorney, bar no., address and telephone no.

TO THE DEFENDANT:

NOTICE

1. Your default was entered on ___4-11-89___, as shown by the attached Default.

2. I will be requesting a default Judgment of Divorce and a hearing on that request is scheduled for ___5-7-89___ at___9:00 AM___ in the courtroom of the judge in this case.

INSERT DATE AND TIME OF THE FINAL HEARING

3. At the hearing, the judge may enter a Judgment of Divorce granting the relief I requested in my Complaint for Divorce and/or grant other relief.

___4-12-89___
Date

Darlene A. Lovelace
Plaintiff signature

PROOF OF MAILING

On the date below, I sent copies of this notice and the Default entered in this case to the defendant, at his/her address in the caption above, by ordinary first-class mail.

I declare that the statement above is true to the best of my information, knowledge and belief.

___4-12-89___
Date

Darlene A. Lovelace
Plaintiff signature

GRP 3   (2/98)   NOTICE OF ENTRY OF DEFAULT AND REQUEST FOR DEFAULT JUDGMENT OF DIVORCE

Request for Certification of Military Status

TO:

Army
Enlisted Records
Fort Benjamin Harrison, IN 46216
Certification fee: $4.50

Navy
World Wide Locator
Bureau of Navy Personnel
PERS-324D
2 Navy Annex
Washington, DC 20370-3240

Marine Corps
Locator Service
USMC-CMC
HQMC-MMSB-10
2008 Elliot Road Suite 210
Quantico, VA 22134-5030
Certification fee: $3.50 (payable to "U.S. Treasurer")

Air Force
World Wide Locator
AFPC MSIMDL
550C Street West Suite 50
Randolph Air Force Base, TX 78150-4752

Coast Guard
Commandant, U.S. Coast Guard
Headquarters, Room 4616
2100 2nd St., S.W.
Washington, DC 22059-0001

RE:

Case name ___LOVELACE V. LOVELACE___

Case number ___89-00501-DO___

Full name of defendant ___DUDLEY ERNEST LOVELACE___

Defendant's social security number ___379-10-5567___

Dates of induction and discharge (if known) _____

I am the plaintiff in the above divorce case, seeking a default judgment of divorce against the defendant. I must know whether or not the defendant is currently in your branch of the U.S. military service, to satisfy the Soldier's and Sailor's Civil Relief Act of 1940.

Please respond with a certificate of the defendant's (non)military status, with dates of induction and discharge, if any, as soon as possible. A self-addressed stamped envelope is enclosed for your response, plus any fee for the certification.

Date ___3-15-89___

Signature ___Darlene A. Lovelace___

Name ___DARLENE A. LOVELACE___

Address ___121 S. MAIN___
___LAKE CITY, MI 48800___

Telephone: ___(517) 772-0000___

4 Final Hearing

The final hearing marks the end of your divorce. This hearing is held in court before the judge assigned to your case. You must attend the hearing and give some brief testimony to support the divorce judgment. Your divorce becomes final immediately after the hearing, when the judgment is filed.

Final Divorce Papers

The final hearing requires some preparation. A few days before the hearing, you should prepare the Judgment of Divorce (GRP 4) and any other final divorce papers you need. The Judgment of Divorce (GRP 4) is by far the most important divorce paper. The judgment ends the marriage, divides property, deals with alimony and may change a wife's name.

Although the Judgment of Divorce (GRP 4) is the court's order, you must prepare it for the court. For guidance, see the sample judgment at the end of this section and the additional judgment provisions in Appendix E.

Besides the Judgment of Divorce (GRP 4), your final divorce papers include the Record of Divorce or Annulment (B 42). You probably got this form from the clerk when you filed the divorce. If not, you can obtain it from the clerk anytime. To prepare the Record of Divorce or Annulment (B 42) for filing, answer questions #1-16 and #19-20. In Wayne County only, you must prepare an extra paper: the Certificate of Conformity for Domestic Relations Order or Judgment (1225). This paper tells the judge that your divorce judgment satisfies all legal requirements.

Preparing Your Testimony

Before you appear in court for your final hearing, you may want to prepare your testimony for the final hearing. Since you won't have a lawyer to ask you questions, you must give the testimony in a monologue. This is a little more difficult than testifying by answering questions. Therefore, you might find it helpful to plan your testimony beforehand.

One way you can do that is by using a script to organize your testimony. By preparing a testimony script, you should be able to memorize the bulk of your testimony. You can also take your testimony script with you to the final hearing and rely on it a bit if your memory fails while you're on the witness stand (using written materials to jog a witness' memory is called "refreshing the recollection," and is permitted by the rules of evidence).

Luckily, the testimony you give during a final hearing is usually quite brief. In most cases, it's simply a repetition of the information contained in the complaint. Some courts even skip the testimony entirely and merely have you swear that the contents of the complaint are true.

You give all the testimony for your hearing; you don't need any testimony from the defendant or other witnesses. In fact, the defendant will probably be absent. Defendants have the right to attend final hearings, but they cannot directly participate because of their default. As a result, defendants seldom attend final hearings in uncontested divorce cases.

On the other hand, in some cases it's beneficial to have the defendant around, if s/he is willing to attend. If your divorce is especially complicated, having the defendant on hand during the final hearing can be helpful to the judge. For example, when you have a complicated property division, the defendant can confirm the arrangement at the final hearing. Defendant-wives who want their names changed must also attend their final hearings to receive name changes.

Preparing for the Final Hearing

When you obtain a judgment at your final hearing, it's a good idea to bring your file with all your divorce papers to the final hearing. If you haven't kept a file, at least bring the following items:

- Judgment of Divorce   GRP 4
    - original
    - 2 copies

- Record of Divorce or Annulment   B 42

- testimony script

[- Certificate of Conformity for Domestic Relations   1225]
    Order or Judgment (in Wayne County only)
    - original
    - 2 copies

Attending the Final Hearing

When you go to the courthouse for the final hearing, arrive early so you can take care of any final details. Clerks often want you to check in with them to let them know that you are present and ready for the final hearing. In some counties, the clerk will give your court file to you to take to the courtroom. But in most counties you won't have to worry about that because the clerk will send your file to the courtroom ahead of time.

You should go to your judge's courtroom before your final hearing is scheduled to begin and wait in the visitor's section in back (see "Court System" on page 48 for more about courts). As your case is called, identify yourself, step forward and take a place at one of the tables. When the judge tells you to proceed, offer your Judgment of Divorce (GRP 4) and say you're ready to give the testimony.

After you take the witness stand and are sworn in, give the testimony as you have planned it. If you omit something important, the judge may ask you some questions to complete the testimony. When your testimony is finished, ask the judge to enter your Judgment of Divorce (GRP 4). If the judgment is satisfactory, the judge will sign the original Judgment of Divorce (GRP 4) and maybe some copies.

If the judge objects to your judgment, s/he should tell you what the problem is. It may be something you can fix on the spot. If not, ask the judge for an opportunity to correct the judgment later. The court rules permit you to submit a corrected judgment to the judge within 14 days after the final hearing. If you get that chance, make any necessary modifications of your Judgment of Divorce (GRP 4) and take it to the judge's office. S/he should sign it there and you won't need another final hearing.

But if something really goes wrong at your final hearing, ask the judge for an adjournment. Find out what the problem is and, after you fix it, reschedule another final hearing. If you reschedule the final hearing, you must also give the defendant notice of the new final hearing in the Notice of Entry of Default and Request for Default Judgment of Divorce (GRP 3). This notice must be given at least seven days before the new final hearing takes place (see "After the Default" on page 74 for more about giving this notice).

Filing the Final Divorce Papers

After the final hearing, file your final divorce papers with the clerk. Filing the papers quickly is important because, according to paragraph #11 of the Judgment of Divorce (GRP 4a), your divorce only becomes final when you file the judgment. At that time, your marriage is ended and all the other provisions of the judgment take effect.

In a few counties, you can file your final divorce papers (and pay the judgment fee) with the courtroom clerk during the final hearing. But in most counties, you must return to the clerk's office, where the clerk will:

■   File the Judgment of Divorce (GRP 4) and return two copies to you.

■   Take the Record of Divorce or Annulment (B 42).

[■   In Wayne County only, file the Certificate of Conformity for Domestic
      Relations Order or Judgment (1225) and return two copies to you.]

After the Final Hearing

Naturally, the defendant must know what the Judgment of Divorce (GRP 4)
says because its provisions affect him/her. After the final hearing, the clerk
should send the defendant a brief notice that a judgment was issued.
However, the clerk doesn't send a copy of the Judgment of Divorce (GRP 4)
itself to the defendant along with this notice. That's your responsibility.

You must send the judgment to the defendant within seven days of the
final hearing. To do that, send a copy of the Judgment of Divorce (GRP 4) to
the defendant by ordinary first-class mail. If the defendant has disappeared,
send it to his/her last known address. After the mailing, prepare the Proof
of Mailing (MC 302) and make two copies. Then file/send the original to the
clerk.

Original - Court
1st copy - Friend of the Court

2nd copy - Defendant
3rd copy - Plaintiff

CASE NO.

STATE OF MICHIGAN
JUDICIAL CIRCUIT - FAMILY DIVISION
COUNTY

JUDGMENT OF DIVORCE
Page 1 of **2** pages

Court telephone no.

Court address

Plaintiff's name, address and social security no.

v

Defendant's name, address and social security no.

Plaintiff's attorney, bar no., address and telephone no.

Defendant's attorney, bar no., address and telephone no.

☐ After trial ☒ Default ☐ Consent

Judge: **LESTER TUBBS**

Date of hearing: **5-7-89**

IT IS ORDERED:

1. **DIVORCE:** The parties are divorced.

2. **MINOR CHILDREN:** There ☐ are ☒ are not children under 18 of the parties or born during this marriage.
   (Custody, parenting time, support and/or other required provisions are attached.)

USE FOR WIFE'S NAME CHANGE

☐ 3. **NAME CHANGE:** Wife's last name is changed to **ALBRIGHT**

4. **SPOUSAL SUPPORT:** Spousal support is
   ☒ not granted for
   ☐ reserved for
   ☐ granted elsewhere in this judgment for

   ☒ wife. ☒ husband.
   ☐ wife. ☐ husband.
   ☐ wife. ☐ husband.

SEE "ALIMONY PROVISIONS" IN APPENDIX E FOR MORE ON SPOUSAL SUPPORT (ALIMONY)

5. **PROPERTY DIVISION:**
   A. **REAL PROPERTY:**
   (Land and buildings)
   ☐ The parties do not own any real property.
   ☒ Real property is divided elsewhere in this judgment.
   ☒ Real property owned by the parties in joint tenancy or tenancy by the entirety is converted to tenancy in co[mmon]

   All real property owned by the parties in his or her possession.
   this judgment provides otherwise.

   B. **PERSONAL PROPERTY:**
   (All other property)
   ☒ Each party is awarded the personal property in his or her possession.
   ☒ Personal property is divided elsewhere in this judgment.

6. **STATUTORY RIGHTS:** All interests of the parties in the property of the [o]ther, now owned or later acquired, including those known as dower under M[CL] 558.1-558.29.
   700.281-700.292, are extinguished, including those known as dower under M[CL]

7. **BENEFICIARY RIGHTS:** The rights each party has to the proceeds or policies [or co]ntracts of li[fe in]surance, endowments, or annuities upon the life of the other as a named beneficiary or by assignment dur[ing]
   ☒ extinguished. ☐ provided for elsewhere in this judgment.

8. **RETIREMENT BENEFITS:** Any rights of either party in any pension, annuity or retir[ement] ☐ provide[d]
   vested or unvested, accumulated or contingent, are ☒ extinguished. ☐ provided for in the[ ]

SEE "PROPERTY DIVISION PROVISIONS" IN APPENDIX E FOR MORE ON PROPERTY DIVISIONS

CHECK BOXES AS THEY APPLY

DOCUMENTATION: Each part[y] [sh]all promptly and properly execute and deliver to the[ ]
A certified [copy] of this judgment may be recorded with the register of d[eeds]

Except as otherwise provided, any nonfinal orders or injunctions [ ]

JUDGMENT: This judgment shall become effective immediately afte[r]

[JUDGM]ENT OF DIVORCE, page 1

SEE "PROPERTY DIVISION PROVISIONS" IN APPENDIX E FOR MORE ON DIVIDING RETIREMENT BENEFITS

Original - Court   2nd copy - Defendant
1st copy - Friend of the Court   3rd copy - Plaintiff

STATE OF MICHIGAN JUDICIAL CIRCUIT - FAMILY DIVISION COUNTY	JUDGMENT OF DIVORCE Final of **2** pages	CASE NO.

Plaintiff   v   Defendant

IT IS FURTHER ORDERED:

12.

13.

ETC.

*INCLUDE
ADDITIONAL JUDGMENT
PROVISIONS
HERE AS NEEDED*

*JUDGE WILL
DATE AND SIGN
AT FINAL
HEARING*

Lester Jubbs
Judge

5-7-89
Date

GRP 4e   (2/98)   JUDGMENT OF DIVORCE, final page

Testimony

1) My name is [full name] , my address is [address], and I am the plaintiff in this case.

2) I was married to the defendant on __SEPT 1, 1985__ at __LAKE CITY, MICHIGAN__ by a person authorized to
Date and place of marriage
perform marriages.

3) Before the marriage, my/[my wife's] name was __DARLENE ANN ALBRIGHT__ .
Wife's former name

4) I filed my complaint for divorce on __MARCH 1, 1989__ . Before I filed the complaint, I had resided in Michigan since
Filing date
__1970__ and in this county since __1970__ .
State residency   *County residency*

5) As I said in my complaint, there has been a breakdown in our marriage relationship to the extent the objects of matrimony
have been destroyed because __WE COULD NEVER GET ALONG TOGETHER__ and there remains no
Brief facts to support grounds
reasonable likelihood that our marriage can be preserved because __WE ARE TOTALLY INCOMPATIBLE__
Brief facts to support grounds

6) The defendant and I have no minor children, and I/[my wife] am not now pregnant.

7) I am working at __A RESTAURANT AS A WAITRESS__ and am able to support myself.
Source of support

8) We own some __CLOTHING AND HOUSEHOLD GOODS__ that we have split between us. We have also agreed that
General description of personal property
the defendant is to give me __A 1984 DODGE ARIES__ worth around __$35,000__ and I will pay off the debt on it.
Specific items of personal property transferred in judgment   *Value*

9) We also own __A HOUSE IN LAKE CITY__
Description of any real property
We have agreed to __SELL IT, PAY OFF THE MORTGAGE AND SPLIT THE REST__
Manner of division

10) I would like my former name of __ALBRIGHT__ back.
Wife's name change

11) My court fees were suspended when I filed this divorce. Since then, __I AM STILL GETTING AFDC AND MY HUSBAND IS UNEMPLOYED__
Current financial condition

12) Does the court have any questions?

USE WHEN APPLICABLE

STATE OF MICHIGAN
THIRD JUDICIAL CIRCUIT
WAYNE COUNTY

Penobscot Bldg. 645 Griswold Ave. Detroit, MI 48226

CERTIFICATE OF CONFORMITY
FOR DOMESTIC RELATIONS
ORDER OR JUDGMENT

CASE NO.

313-224-5372

PLAINTIFF'S NAME

V.

DEFENDANT'S NAME

I certify the attached Order or Judgment as presented for entry to be in full conformity with the requirements set forth by statute, INCLUDING A PROVISION FOR IMMEDIATE INCOME WITHHOLDING (WHICH SHALL BE IMPLEMENTED BY THE FRIEND OF THE COURT), THE PAYER'S SOCIAL SECURITY NUMBER AND THE NAME AND ADDRESS OF HIS/HER SOURCE OF INCOME IF KNOWN , UNLESS OTHERWISE ORDERED BY THE COURT, and with Michigan Court Rules 3.201 and following, and if applicable, includes all provisions of the Friend of the Court recommendation or is in conformity with the decision of

_____

_____ rendered on the _____ day of

_____ , 19 _____ .

5-5-89
Date

Darlene A. Lovelace
Attorney / Bar No.
PLAINTIFF

Instructions : Please sign and present this Certificate to the Court Clerk when the Order or Judgment is presented for entry. If an ex parte interim order is being presented to the Judge, please complete the "Certificate on Behalf of Plaintiff regarding Ex Parte Interim Support Order" and follow Local Court Rule 3.206.

#1225 (7/95) CERTIFICATE OF CONFORMITY FOR DOMESTIC RELATIONS ORDER OR JUDGMENT

Approved, SCAO

CASE NO.

STATE OF MICHIGAN
JUDICIAL DISTRICT
JUDICIAL CIRCUIT

PROOF OF MAILING

Court telephone no.

Court address

Plaintiff(s)

Defendant(s)

v

On the date below I sent by first class mail a copy of ———— JUDGMENT OF DIVORCE

to: Names and addresses

DUDLEY LOVELACE
900 S. MAPLE
LAKE CITY, MI 48800

I declare that the statements above are true to the best of my information, knowledge and belief.

DARLENE A. LOVELACE
Name (typed)

5-8-89
Date

Darlene A. Lovelace
Signature

MC 302 (5/88) PROOF OF MAILING

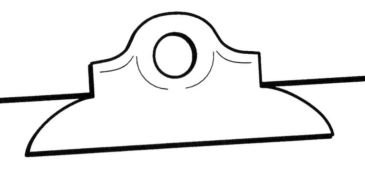

3 Default

Filed with the clerk when default is received:

GRP 2

☐ Default

[☐ praecipe or other written request for final hearing]

Filed with clerk after default:

☐ Notice of Entry of Default and Request for Default Judgment   GRP 3
of Divorce

4 Final Hearing

Filed with the clerk after the final hearing:

GRP 4

☐ Judgment of Divorce

B 42

☐ Record of Divorce or Annulment

[☐ Certificate of Conformity for Domestic Relations Order or   1225]
Judgment (in Wayne County only)

Filed with the clerk after service of the final papers on the defendant:

MC 302

☐ Proof of Mailing

After Your Divorce

Although your divorce is over, there's still some work to do. The Judgment of Divorce (GRP 4) takes legal effect at filing, but you must carry out several of its provisions. What's more, the end of your marriage may require changes in your will, powers of attorney, insurance, retirement benefits, etc.

Transferring Property

The Judgment of Divorce (GRP 4) divided your property, but it's your responsibility to transfer ownership of the property.

Ownership of real property must be transferred by deed. For transfers between ex-spouses, a simple form of deed called a quit claim deed is customarily used. Lawyers or real estate brokers can prepare these for a small fee.

If your ex-spouse is uncooperative or unavailable for transfer, you can sometimes use the divorce judgment to transfer ownership of real property yourself. To use the judgment this way, it must describe the property in detail (see "Property Division Provisions" in Appendix E for more about describing property using legal descriptions or identification numbers). You must also have an official certified copy of the judgment for the transfer. These are available from the clerk for a small fee.

You can transfer Michigan real property by recording a certified copy of the divorce judgment with the register of deeds for the county where the property is located. This transfer method isn't available for out-of-state real property.

Personal property without titles (clothing, household goods, etc.) can be transferred by simply changing possession of the items. But both possession and title must be transferred for personal property with titles (stocks, bonds, motor vehicles, etc.). Stocks and bonds can be transferred through the designated transfer agent (usually a bank but sometimes the issuing company itself).

Transfer titles to motor vehicles through a secretary of state office by applying for a new title after the current owner has signed off on the back of the old certificate of title.

If the owner refuses to cooperate, you can use a certified copy of the divorce judgment for transfer of title. When you apply for a new title, submit a certified copy of the judgment, and you won't need your ex's signature on the old certificate of title.

Debts

You may have already closed or frozen joint accounts (see "Does My Property Need Protection?" on page 34 for more about handling joint accounts during divorce). If you haven't, do this at once. Otherwise, your ex can add new joint debt after the divorce for which you may be liable.

Estate Planning

Paragraphs #7 and #8 of the Judgment of Divorce (GRP 4a) end all claims you and your ex-spouse have against each other's life insurance and retirement benefits (unless you provided otherwise elsewhere in the judgment).

Despite these provisions, you should contact your insurance agent and/or retirement plan administrator and revoke any designations of your spouse as beneficiary. Because of a legal peculiarity, a divorce judgment's revocations aren't always effective, making individual revocation necessary. As you make the revocation, it's a good time to make new beneficiary designations.

Paragraph #6 of the Judgment of Divorce (GRP 4a) cuts off all rights that spouses have in their partners' estates (see "Do I Really Want to End My Marriage?" on page 19 for a description of these rights). And although the judgment doesn't mention it, Michigan law says that divorce automatically revokes: 1) all rights that spouses have been given in each other's will 2) an appointment of a spouse as personal representative.

But besides those selected will provisions, divorce doesn't touch any other parts of a will. The will, minus the provisions benefiting an ex-spouse, remains in force. All the same, you should carefully review your will after divorce. The removal of your ex-spouse from the will may have upset your scheme of property distribution and appointments. After review, you may decide that your will needs revision or even replacement.

These days, some people have living (*inter vivos*) trusts instead of wills. If you have one, with your ex as trustee and/or beneficiary, you'll probably want to amend the trust and remove your ex.

You might have already revoked your financial power of attorney with your ex-spouse as agent. If not, you may want to revoke it now. Simply give or send a written notice telling your ex that you are revoking the power of attorney and his/her powers under it. Make sure you keep a copy of the revocation.

In 1990, Michigan created a special health care power of attorney allowing you to designate an agent, called a patient advocate, to make health care decisions, including the termination of life-sustaining treatment, on your behalf. Like financial powers of attorney, spouses who make these arrangements often name each other as patient advocates.

The health care power of attorney law helpfully provides that a designation of a spouse as patient advocate is suspended while a divorce is pending. Then, when the divorce judgment is filed, the health care power of attorney is automatically revoked, unless you named a successor patient advocate. In that case, the power of attorney remains in effect with the successor as patient advocate.

Health Care Coverage

With the high cost of health care these days, health care coverage is vital. If you want to obtain health insurance through your ex-spouse's employer as permitted by COBRA (see "Do I Really Want to End My Marriage?" on page 19 for more about this right), contact his/her employee benefits office within 60 days after your judgment is granted. If you wait longer, you may lose the right to obtain health insurance this way.

Name Change

If you changed your name during the divorce, you should apply to the: 1) secretary of state for a new driver's license 2) social security office for a new social security card. When you apply for these documents, bring photocopies of the Judgment of Divorce (GRP 4) as proof of your name change.

Credit Problems

After divorce, many women suddenly discover that they can't get credit because they have no credit history. A woman may lose credit if her credit was reported in her previous married name. Even women who don't change their names may suffer a loss of credit if they got credit through their husbands' credit files.

The solution to these credit woes is building a credit file in your own name. If you had credit under your former married name, you can add this information to your credit file. Joint

More Information

To check on your credit status, get copies of your credit reports from the three main credit reporting agencies:

Equifax: 1-800-685-1111
Experian: 1-800-682-7654
Trans Union Corp.: 1-800-916-8800

More Information

Ask for "Women and Credit Histories" and "Equal Credit Opportunity" from:

Federal Trade Commission
Attn: Ed Bush
6th & Pennsylvania Ave. N.W.
Washington, DC 20580

accounts with your husband may have been reported in your husband's name only (all joint accounts opened after June 1, 1977, are supposed to be reported in both spouses' names). If so, you can sometimes persuade credit reporting agencies to add these credit references to your file.

In addition, you can apply for new credit from banks, department stores and other creditors to build up your credit file. A federal law, the Equal Credit Opportunity Act (ECOA), forbids creditors from canceling old credit accounts you had during marriage if you still meet their lending standards (you may have to submit new information to prove your creditworthiness). The ECOA also guarantees creditworthy persons access to credit regardless of sex or marital status, and outlaws various discriminatory credit practices.

Appendices

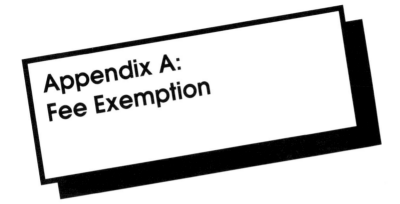

Appendix A: Fee Exemption

Michigan law exempts some poor people from payment of the court fees of their divorces (see "How Much Will My Divorce Cost?" on page 28 for a description of these fees). If you qualify, you can get an exemption from payment of the filing fee and any motion fees. You can also get an exemption from the service fee when you must use: 1) an official server (such as a sheriff for service by delivery; or a sheriff, policeman or court officer for alternate service by posting) 2) publication for alternate service. Otherwise, you must pay the service fee yourself for service by mail or service by delivery using a commercial process server.

Who can qualify for a fee exemption? The court rules say that persons receiving "any form of public assistance" are automatically entitled to a fee exemption. The rules don't define public assistance, but presumably it includes the main public welfare programs: 1) Aid to Families with Dependent Children (AFDC) 2) Medicaid 3) food stamps 4) General Assistance (GA) 5) Supplemental Security Income (SSI).

In addition, the court rules say that indigent persons may qualify for fee exemptions. Indigent is just another word for poor. In Michigan, judges determine indigency on a case-by-case basis after they have reviewed applicants' financial information.

The fee exemption rules apply to all types of lawsuits, but there is a special rule for divorce cases. Although you and your spouse may be separated and financially independent, you're still treated as a family unit for fee exemption purposes. If you cannot pay the fees, but your spouse can, s/he may be ordered to pay them for you. If neither of you can pay the fees, because of: 1) receipt of public assistance 2) indigency, both of you are exempt from payment.

Obtaining a Fee Exemption

Obtaining a fee exemption is a two-step procedure: 1) initial suspension of fees when a divorce is filed 2) final exemption (or payment) of the fees at the end of the divorce. To get fees suspended initially, prepare the Affidavit section of the Affidavit and Order, Suspension of Fees/Costs (MC 20), and submit it to the clerk when you file your initial divorce papers. You don't have to pay the normal $20 motion fee for a fee exemption request.

The clerk gives automatic fee exemptions to those receiving public assistance. If you claim indigency, the clerk will pass the Affidavit and Order, Suspension of Fees/Costs (MC 20) on to the judge for review. If the judge agrees that you're indigent, s/he will order a fee suspension on the reverse of the Affidavit and Order, Suspension of Fees/Costs (MC 20). A denial of your application would be indicated in the same place.

If your application is successful, you won't have to pay any fees during your divorce. However, the court will review your fee exemption at the end of the divorce. At that time, it will take another look at your financial condition and make a final decision about the fees.

During your testimony at the final hearing, you must mention that your fees were suspended at the beginning of the divorce. The judge will then re-examine your financial condition and either: 1) give you and your spouse a final exemption from payment of the fees or 2) order you or your spouse to pay the fees. The same standards apply then as before. Those on public assistance get an automatic exemption, while those claiming indigency must cite facts to prove it. To prove indigency, you should give extra testimony about your present financial condition.

If the judge finds that neither you nor your spouse can pay the fees, s/he will order a final exemption. But if either of you is now able to pay, the judge will order payment. If that happens, you must add a fee payment provision to your Judgment of Divorce (GRP 4e), like this:

12. <u>Court Fees.</u> Defendant shall immediately pay the suspended court fees of [$100] to the court clerk.

Original - Court
1st copy - Applicant
2nd copy - Opposing party
PROBATE OSM CODE: OSF

CASE NO.

Approved, SCAO

STATE OF MICHIGAN
JUDICIAL DISTRICT
JUDICIAL CIRCUIT
COUNTY PROBATE

AFFIDAVIT AND ORDER
SUSPENSION OF FEES/COSTS

Court telephone no.

Court address

Plaintiff/Petitioner name, address, and telephone no.

Defendant/Respondent name, address, and telephone no.

v

Plaintiff's/Petitioner's attorney, bar no., address, and telephone no.

Defendant's/Respondent's attorney, bar no., address, and telephone no.

COMPLETE 2a. IF YOU ARE RECEIVING PUBLIC ASSISTANCE

...tter of _____

AFFIDAVIT DARLENE A. LOVELACE
Name

...ing is to be filed with the court by or on behalf of

applicant,   is ☒ plaintiff/petitioner.   ☐ defendant/respondent.

2. The applican... is entitled to and asks the court for suspension of fees and costs in the action for the following reason:

☒ a. S/he is currently receiving public assistance: $ **400** per **MONTH** Case No.: **U1336092B**

COMPLETE 2b. INSTEAD IF YOU ARE CLAIMING INDIGENCY

☒ b. S/he is unable to pay those fees and costs because of indigency, based on the following facts:

INCOME: **10,000 PANCAKES, 111 M-78, LAKE CITY, MI 48800**
Employer name and address

$250   **$225**   per ☒ week. ☐ month.
Average gross pay   Average net pay

1 YR.
Length of employment

ASSETS: State value of car, home, bank deposits, bonds, stocks, etc.   **HOUSEHOLD GOODS $1,000**
                                                                        CAR $1,000

OBLIGATIONS: Itemize monthly rent, installment payments, mortgage payments, child support, etc.
CAR PAYMENT $75
RENT $250
FOOD $200

REIMBURSEMENT:
3. (in domestic relations cases only) The applicant is entitled to an order requiring his/her spouse to pay attorney fees.

Darlene A. Lovelace
Affiant signature

Subscribed and sworn to before me on **2-28-89**   **OJIBWAY**   Cou...
Date

My commission expires: **1-1-90**   Signature: *Loretta Smiley*
Date   Deputy clerk/Register/Notary public

IF YOU MUST USE AN OFFICIAL SERVER, OR MUST GET ALTERNATE SERVICE BY PUBLICATION, EXPLAIN THAT ON A SHEET ATTACHED TO THIS FORM

(SEE REVERSE SIDE FOR ORDER)

MC 20 (9/95) **AFFIDAVIT AND ORDER, SUSPENSION OF FEES/COSTS**

CERTIFICATION OF ATTORNEY

1. I have reviewed the affidavit of indigency, and I certify that its contents are true to the best of my information, knowledge, and belief.

2. I will bring to the court's attention the matter of suspended costs and fees and the availability of funds to pay them before any disposition is entered. I will report at that time any changes in the information contained in the affidavit of indigency or any other information regarding the affiant's financial status or alterations of the fee arrangement.

Date _____

Attorney signature _____

Attorney name (type or print) _____

Bar no. _____

CERTIFICATION BY PERSON OTHER THAN PARTY

1. I have personal knowledge of the facts appearing in the affidavit.

2. The person in whose behalf the petition is filed is unable to sign it because of

☐ minority: _____
Date of birth

Relationship: _____   ☐ other disability: _____

Nature of disability

LEAVE CERTIFICATIONS BLANK

Date _____

Affiant signature _____

Affiant name (type or print) _____

Address _____

City, state, zip _____

IT IS ORDERED:

JUDGE WILL SUSPEND FEES OR DENY FEE SUSPENSION BELOW

ORDER

Telephone no. _____

☒ 1. Fees and costs in this action required by law or court rule are waived/suspended until further order of the court. Before any final disposition or discontinuance is entered, the moving party shall bring the fee and costs suspension to the attention of the judge for final disposition.

2. Requests for waiver/suspension of transcript costs must be made separately by motion.

☐ 3. The applicant's spouse shall pay the fees and costs required by law or court rule.

☐ 4. This application is denied.

Date 3-1-89

Judge *Lester Jublas*

Bar no. _____

JUDGE WILL DATE AND SIGN

Appendix B:
Alternate Service

The regular service methods of service by acknowledgment, mail and delivery are effective when defendants are available for service. But if the defendant is eluding or hiding from service (an elusive defendant), or has disappeared entirely (a disappeared defendant), you must do something else. Luckily, the court rules authorize alternate service on elusive and disappeared defendants. By using alternate service, your divorce can go ahead normally, just as if you had served the defendant by one of the regular service methods.

Alternate service can take several forms including: 1) mailing 2) tacking (attaching papers to a door) 3) household delivery (delivering papers to an adult in the defendant's household) 4) publication (with or without an accompanying registered mailing) 5) posting (with or without an accompanying registered mailing) 6) any combination of these things 7) something different.

The judge picks from among these options to devise a method of alternate service for the defendant. The method is designed to give the defendant *actual* notice of the divorce. But if the alternate service doesn't give actual notice, that's all right. Elusive and disappeared defendants are legally entitled to whatever notice alternate service provides, even if this means no actual notice.

When the defendant is elusive, the judge will probably order either mailing, tacking, household delivery, or a combination of them. But all these methods won't work on disappeared defendants. For them, judges normally order publication or posting. With either method, judges can order registered mailing of the service papers to the defendant's last known address. But if that address appears to be outdated, the judge can skip the mailing and order publication or posting alone.

Whatever form alternate service takes, keep in mind that you cannot perform it yourself because you're disqualified from serving as a party to the divorce. As with regular service, you must have a server—a helper or professional server—to carry out alternate service. You can apply for and help with the alternate service, but the helper or server must serve the service papers for you (see "Preparing for Service" on page 62 for which papers make up your service papers).

Alternate Service for an Elusive Defendant

With an elusive defendant, you know his/her home and/or business address. Before you apply for alternate service, you must try service by delivery on the defendant at those or other places. For service by delivery, use the procedure described in "Service by Delivery" on page 66. Since the service will probably be difficult, use a professional server, such as a sheriff or commercial process server. Tell the server to attempt delivery not once but three or four times.

You must also ask the server to describe each attempt in the Verification of Process Server section of the Motion and Verification for Alternate Service (MC 303), which you should give to the server along with the service papers. The server's description of each delivery attempt must include specific information about the date, place and outcome of the attempt, as shown in the sample form at the end of this appendix.

If the server succeeds in serving the defendant during those attempts, you have obtained service on the defendant by delivery, and don't need alternate service. But if service by delivery fails, the server will return the service papers to you and you can apply for alternate service.

Make sure that the server has completed the Verification of Process Server section in the Motion and Verification for Alternate Service (MC 303), and then pay the server for the attempted service. You must complete the top portion of the Motion and Verification for Alternate Service (MC 303), above the verification section. Because you are trying to serve an elusive defendant, complete paragraph #2a of the motion showing that you know the defendant's current home and/or business address. You should also complete the caption and paragraph #1 of the Order for Alternate Service (MC 304), and return to the clerk with:

- Motion and Verification for Alternate Service   MC 303
  - original
  - one copy

- Order for Alternate Service   MC 304
  - original

- $20 motion fee

File the Motion and Verification for Alternate Service (MC 303) with the clerk. After filing, go to your judge's office and submit a copy of the Motion and Verification for Alternate Service (MC 303) and the original Order for Alternate Service (MC 304) to the judge's secretary. The judge will review your motion in his/her office (although probably not while you wait), so a court hearing on the motion won't be necessary. If the judge grants your motion for alternate service, get the papers back from the judge's office and make three photocopies of the Order for Alternate Service (MC 304). Return to the clerk and file the original.

Examine the Order for Alternate Service (MC 304) to see which form of alternate service the judge has designed for the defendant. It will probably be either mailing, tacking, household delivery, or a combination of them. (If the judge has ordered several things, prepare multiple sets of the service papers and the Order for Alternate Service (MC 304) because you will need separate sets of these papers for each form of alternate service ordered.) However, the judge could order another form of alternate service, which would be described in paragraph #2d. If the judge orders publication or posting, see the sections on these methods below.

Mailing

For this type of mailing, ordinary first-class mailing is permissible. Have your helper or server mail the service papers and a copy of the Order for Alternate Service (MC 304) to the person named by the judge in paragraph #2a of the order. The recipient might be the defendant or a friend or relative. The day of service is the day the mailing is sent, not received. After the mailing is sent, have the helper or server complete paragraph #1 in the Proof of Service section on the reverse of one of your copies of the Order for Alternate Service (MC 304).

Tacking

When tacking has been ordered, have your helper or server take the service papers and a copy of the Order for Alternate Service (MC 304) to the address indicated at paragraph #2b of the order, and attach them to the front door at this address. The day of service is the day the papers are tacked to the door. After tacking, the helper or server must complete paragraph #2 in the Proof of Service section on the reverse of the copy of the Order for Alternate Service (MC 304) that you're using for proof of service.

Household Delivery

To use this service method, your helper or server takes the service papers and a copy of the Order for Alternate Service (MC 304) to the defendant's house and delivers them to any adult living there. The helper or server must also tell that person to give the papers to the defendant. The day of service is the day the papers are delivered to the person in defendant's household. After delivery, the helper or server must prove service on the reverse of your proof of service copy of the Order for Alternate Service (MC 304). In this case, proof of the household delivery is made in paragraph #3 in the Proof of Service section of that paper.*

Alternate Service for a Disappeared Defendant

If you don't know the current home or business address of the defendant, you might be able to convince the court that the defendant has disappeared and obtain alternate service by publication or posting. But before you ask for that, you must prove the defendant's disappearance by searching for his/her current home and business addresses. To search for these, try several of the following things:

¶ When you know the city or state where the defendant lives, use the following local resources:
  - *Telephone company.* Check the telephone book or call directory assistance.
  - *Library.* Most libraries have city directories, such as Polk's or Bresser's, with information about residents' home and business addresses. Libraries may also have telephone books or master telephone directories on CD-ROM, such as PhoneDisc, with everyone in the United States with a listed telephone number.
  - *Michigan Bureau of Driver and Vehicle Records.* For a small fee, you can get the current address for anyone licensed to drive in the state. Call (517) 322-1624 during business hours.
  - *Voter registration office.* The city or township clerk will have record of the defendant's address if s/he is registered to vote.
  - *Michigan Bureau of Occupational and Professional Regulation.* For a small fee, you can find out if someone is licensed to practice a trade or profession in the state and obtain the person's business address. Call 1-900-740-6111 during business hours.

¶ Contact the defendant's relatives, friends, former neighbors, landlords and employers to see if they know where s/he is.

¶ If the defendant is a student at or graduate of a college or university, check the school's student or alumni directory.

¶ Use the U.S. Postal Service to hunt for the defendant's address:
  - For a small fee, the postal service will provide you with the defendant's current forwarding address. Apply at the post office in the defendant's last known zip code.

---

*   After service by mailing, tacking or household delivery has been proved on the reverse of a copy of the Order for Alternate Service (MC 304), make two copies of this paper and save for filing later as your proof of service.

- An address verification can take several weeks. You can sometimes obtain the defendant's forwarding address faster by sending a letter to the defendant's last known address. Write "Address Correction Requested - Return Postage Guaranteed" on the envelope. When the letter is returned to you, pay the postage for the return and see if a new address is marked on the envelope.

¶ If the defendant is overseas, you may be able to find him/her through the U.S. Department of State:

(1) Contact the state department's Passport Services and see if the defendant's passport contains an overseas destination and maybe even an address. Write the passport services at:

> Passport Services
> Research and Liaison Branch
> 111 19th St. N.W.
> Suite 200
> Washington, DC 20522

(2) After you locate the country where the defendant is living, contact the U.S. embassy in the country. The embassy can often request the foreign country to provide the defendant's current address there. For help with these embassy requests, contact the U.S. Department of State at (202) 647-4000.

During your search for the defendant, keep a written record of when and what you did. For example, if you contact relatives or friends of the defendant, record the date, person with whom you spoke and what s/he said. Keep any written evidence of your attempts to find the defendant, such as undelivered letters to him/her or correspondence with others about the defendant's disappearance. All this information is valuable because you will use it later when you apply for alternate service.

If you happen to find the defendant's home and/or business address during your search, attempt service on him/her using one of the regular service methods.* But if you fail to discover the defendant's whereabouts during your search, your failure will show that the defendant has disappeared, allowing you to apply for alternate service by publication or posting.

Complete the top portion of the Motion and Verification for Alternate Service (MC 303) above the Verification of Process Server section, which you can leave blank. Since you're trying to serve a disappeared defendant, complete paragraph #2b of the motion showing that you don't know the defendant's current home and business addresses. After you complete the Motion and Verification for Alternate Service (MC 303), attach any written

---

* If you discover the defendant's current home or business address, but fail to have him/her served there, see above on serving an elusive defendant.

materials (undelivered letters, correspondence with the defendant's friends and relatives, etc.) which show that you failed to discover the defendant's whereabouts. Then complete the caption and first two lines of the Order for Service by Publication/Posting and Notice of Action (MC 307). After you prepare these papers, return to the clerk with:

- Motion and Verification for Alternate Service   MC 303
    - original
    - one copy

- Order for Service by Publication/Posting and Notice of Action   MC 307
    - original

- $20 motion fee

File the Motion and Verification for Alternate Service (MC 303) with the clerk. After filing, go to your judge's office and submit a copy of the Motion and Verification for Alternate Service (MC 303) and the original Order for Service by Publication/Posting and Notice of Action (MC 307) to the judge's secretary. The judge will review your motion in his/her office (although probably not while you wait), so a court hearing on the motion won't be necessary. If the judge grants your motion for alternate service, get the papers back from the judge's office and make two photocopies of the Order for Service by Publication/Posting and Notice of Action (MC 307). Return to the clerk and file the original.

Examine the Order for Service by Publication/Posting and Notice of Action (MC 307) to see which form of alternate service the judge has devised for the defendant. It's probably either publication (paragraph #2) or posting (paragraph #3), and possibly a registered mailing (paragraph #4). If registered mailing has been ordered, make an extra photocopy of the Order for Service by Publication/Posting and Notice of Action (MC 307).

Publication

If the judge has ordered publication as the alternate service in your case, you must publish a legal advertisement in a newspaper. Maybe you have seen fine-print legal advertisements in newspapers. These are advertisements like the one you must place.

The court rules say that the legal advertisement must be published in a newspaper in the county where the defendant resides when you know the defendant's residence. If you don't know where the defendant is residing, the court rules permit advertisement in the county where the case is filed. Since your defendant has disappeared, you can advertise in the county where you filed for divorce, which is probably your county.

See which newspaper the judge has chosen as the publisher of your advertisement in paragraph #2 of the Order for Service by Publication/Posting and Notice of Action (MC 307). Take/send a copy of the Order for Service by Publication/Posting and Notice of Action (MC 307) to that newspaper and ask it to prepare a legal advertisement for you. The newspaper will create an advertisement using the caption and paragraph #1 of the Order for Service by Publication/Posting and Notice of Action (MC 307). It will publish the advertisement as instructed in paragraph #2 of the order. Ordinarily, publication must be once a week for three consecutive weeks.

Once the advertisement has been published the required number of times, the newspaper will bill you for the cost of publication.* After you pay the bill, the newspaper will complete the Affidavit of Publishing on the reverse of the copy of the Order for Service by Publication/Posting and Notice of Action (MC 307) that you gave it and return this paper to you.

If the defendant's last known address is old, the judge will probably omit registered mailing of the service papers to the defendant. But if the defendant's last known address is fairly recent, registered mailing may be required.

If the judge has ordered registered mailing, have a helper mail the service papers and a copy of the Order for Service by Publication/Posting and Notice of Action (MC 307) to the defendant at his/her last known address. This mailing must be by registered (not certified) mail, return receipt requested. The mailing must be sent sometime before the date of the last publication of the legal advertisement.

Afterward, have your helper complete the Affidavit of Mailing on the reverse of a copy of the Order for Service by Publication/Posting and Notice of Action (MC 307), and attach both the Receipt for Registered Mail (PS Form 3806) and the Domestic Return Receipt (PS Form 3811), signed or unsigned, to it. Your helper can use the Affidavit of Mailing on the same copy of the Order for Service by Publication/Posting and Notice of Action (MC 307) that the newspaper used to prove publication, or you can use another copy. Either way, make two copies of the reverse of the order(s) and save for filing later as your proof of service.

Posting

Judges seem to prefer publication as the method of alternate service for disappeared defendants, and posting is seldom ordered. But if posting was ordered in your Order for Service by Publication/Posting and Notice of Action (MC 307), look at paragraph #3 to see who was designated as the poster. That person might be a sheriff, policeman or court official, such as a

---

* The cost of your advertisement depends on its size and the frequency of publication. Since you really only need to publish the caption and paragraph #1 of the Order for Service by Publication/Posting and Notice of Action (MC 307), your advertisement should not be large. The newspaper may want to print the entire order, but that is unnecessary and will cost you more. Your advertisement will probably be published three times. In that case, there is a minimum charge of around $45, but the cost will probably be slightly more, perhaps $50-100.

bailiff. Take four copies of the Order for Service by Publication/Posting and Notice of Action (MC 307) to the person designated as the poster and request posting of the order. The poster will post the order in the courthouse and the two other public places the court has specified in paragraph #3. Ordinarily, the order will remain posted for three consecutive weeks. After the posting period expires, the poster will bill you for posting and prove the posting in the Affidavit of Posting on the reverse of the extra copy of the Order for Service by Publication/Posting and Notice of Action (MC 307).

Like alternate service by publication, alternate service by posting can be with or without registered mailing of the service papers to the defendant. If the judge has ordered registered mailing in paragraph #4 of the Order for Service by Publication/Posting and Notice of Action (MC 307), have your helper mail the service papers and a copy of the Order for Service by Publication/Posting and Notice of Action (MC 307) to the defendant at his/her last known address. This mailing should be made by registered (not certified) mail, return receipt requested. The mailing must be sent sometime before the last week of the posting.

Afterward, have your helper complete the Affidavit of Mailing on the reverse of a copy of the Order for Service by Publication/Posting and Notice of Action (MC 307), and attach both the Receipt for Registered Mail (PS Form 3806) and the Domestic Return Receipt (PS Form 3811), signed or unsigned, to it. Your helper can complete the Affidavit of Mailing on the same copy of the Order for Service by Publication/Posting and Notice of Action (MC 307) that the poster used to prove posting, or you can use another copy. Either way, make two copies of the reverse of the order(s) and save for filing later as your proof of service.

Original - Court
1st copy - Serving party
2nd copy - Extra

CASE NO.

Approved, SCAO

STATE OF MICHIGAN
JUDICIAL DISTRICT
JUDICIAL CIRCUIT

**MOTION AND VERIFICATION
FOR ALTERNATE SERVICE**

Court telephone no.

Court address

Defendant name(s), address(es), and telephone number(s)

Plaintiff name(s), address(es), and telephone number(s)

v

_____ cannot reasonably be made as

1. Service of process upon _**DUDLEY E. LOVELACE**_ otherwise provided in MCR 2.105, as shown in the following verification of process server.

2. Defendant's last known home and business addresses are:

900 S. MAPLE   **LAKE CITY**   **MI**   **48800**
Home address   City   State   Zip

1000 SERVICE RD.   "   "   "
Business address   City   State   Zip

*COMPLETE 2b.
INSTEAD FOR A
DISAPPEARED
DEFENDANT*

  a. I believe the ☒ home   address shown above is current.
            ☒ business

  b. I do not know defendant's current ☒ home   address. I have made the following efforts to ascertain the
                              ☒ business
  current address: **3-4-89 SEARCHED TELEPHONE AND CITY DIRECTORIES/
3-7-89 CALLED SECRETARY OF STATE/3-7-89 REQUESTED CHANGE OF
ADDRESS FROM USPS/3-7-89 WROTE TO MABEL LOVELACE (MOTHER) (SEE
ATTACHED LETTER); ALL TO NO AVAIL.**

*COMPLETE
2a. FOR AN
ELUSIVE
DEFENDANT*

I request the court order service by alternate means.

I declare that the statements above are true to the best of my information, knowledge and belief.

Darlene A. Lovelace
Attorney signature   Bar no.

3-15-89
Date   Attorney name (type or print)

Address

City, state, zip   Telephone no.

VERIFICATION OF PROCESS SERVER

1. I have tried to serve process on this defendant as described: State date, place, and what occurred on each occasion

3-4-89 TRIED TO SERVE DEFENDANT AT 900 S. MAPLE, LAKE CITY, MI; BUT A WOMAN THERE TOLD ME DEFENDANT WAS NOT AT HOME WHEN IT APPEARED HE WAS.

3-5-89 " TRIED TO SERVE DEFENDANT AT 1000 SERVICE RD., LAKE CITY, MI; BUT
3-6-89 " HIS EMPLOYER PREVENTED SERVICE.
3-7-89 TRIED TO SERVE DEFENDANT AT 1000 SERVICE RD, LAKE CITY, MI; BUT
3-8-89 TRIED TO SERVE DEFENDANT AT 1000 SERVICE RD., LAKE CITY, MI; BUT HE SPED AWAY IN HIS CAR.

I declare that the statements above are true to the best of my information, knowledge and belief.

Chester Gunn
Signature

3-14-89   **CHESTER GUNN**
Date   Process Server (type or print)   MCR 2.105

*SERVER MUST
COMPLETE VERIFICATION
OF PROCESS SERVER FOR
ATTEMPTED SERVICE ON
AN ELUSIVE
DEFENDANT*

MOTION AND VERIFICATION FOR ALTERNATE SERVICE

MC 303 (6/

Approved, SCAO

STATE OF MICHIGAN JUDICIAL DISTRICT JUDICIAL CIRCUIT	ORDER FOR ALTERNATE SERVICE	Original - Court 2nd copy - Plaintiff 1st copy - Defendant 3rd copy - Return
Court address		CASE NO.

Plaintiff name(s), address(es), and telephone no.(s)		Court telephone no.
	v	Defendant name(s), address(es), and telephone no.(s)
Plaintiff's attorney, bar no., address, and telephone no.		

THE COURT FINDS:

1. Service of process upon defendant _____DUDLEY E. LOVELACE_____ cannot reasonably be made as provided in MCR 2.105, and service of process may be made in a manner which is reasonably calculated to give defendant actual notice of the proceedings and an opportunity to be heard.

IT IS ORDERED:

2. Service of the summons and complaint and a copy of this order may be made by the following method(s):

a. ☒ First class mail to _____900 S. MAPLE, LAKE CITY, MI_____

b. ☒ Tacking or firmly affixing to the door at _____ "

c. ☒ Delivering at _____ "

to a member of defendant's household who is of suitable age and discretion to receive process, with instructions to deliver it promptly to defendant.

d. ☐ Other: _____

_____

3. For each method used, proof of service must be filed promptly with the court.

_____3-17-89_____
Date

_____Lester Tubbs_____
Judge

MC 304 (8/88)   ORDER FOR ALTERNATE SERVICE

Bar no.

MCR 2.103, MCR 2.105

JUDGE WILL CHOOSE ONE OR MORE OF THESE METHODS

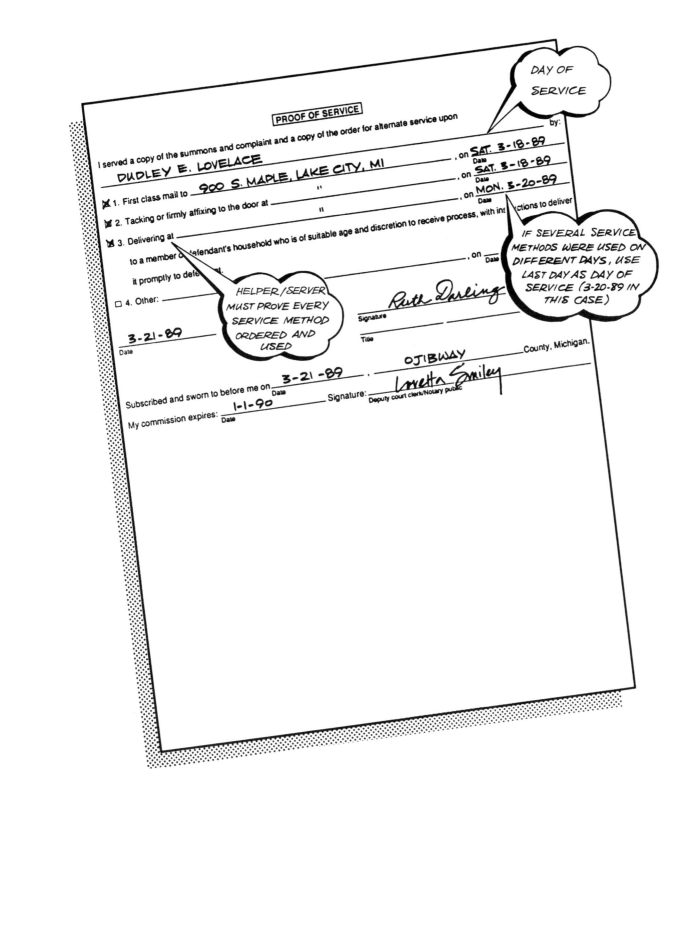

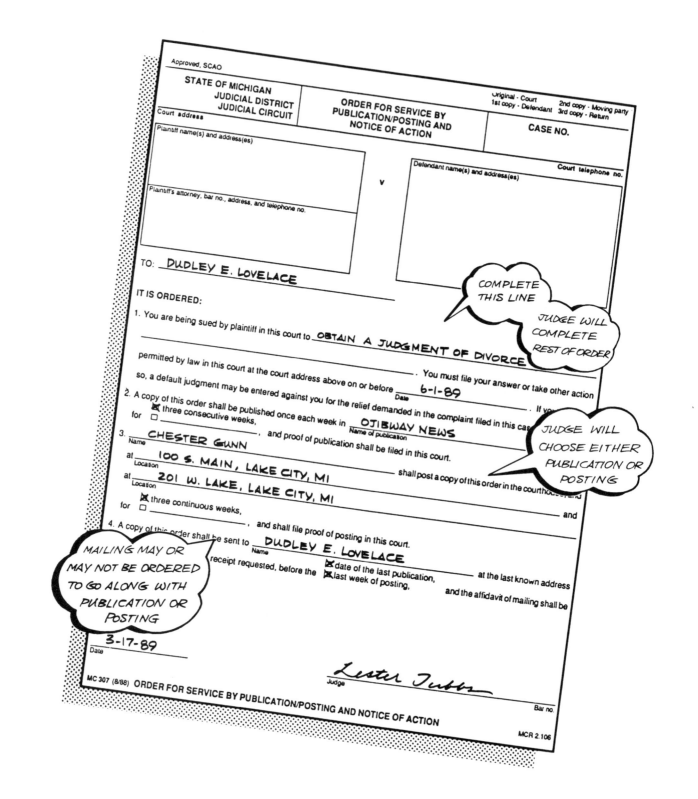

AFFIDAVIT OF PUBLISHING

Attach copy of publication here

NEWSPAPER WILL ATTACH A COPY OF THE ADVERTISEMENT

Name of ☒ publisher ☐ agent of publisher

ELTON BEAN

County where published OJIBWAY

Name of newspaper OJIBWAY NEWS

This newspaper is a qualified newspaper. The attached copy was published in this newpaper for at least 3 consecutive weeks on these dates:

3-25-89, 4-1-89, 4-8-89

4-15-89

Elton Bean
Affiant signature

Date

sworn to before me on ___ Date 4-15-89

OJIBWAY ___ County, Michigan.

Signature: *Loretta Smiley*
Court clerk/Notary public

...pires: 1-1-90
Date

NEWSPAPER WILL COMPLETE

POSTER WILL COMPLETE

AFFIDAVIT OF POSTING

OJIBWAY COUNTY ___ courthouse and the

I have posted this order in a conspicuous place in the

following places as ordered by this court: 100 S. MAIN AND 201 W. LAKE, LAKE CITY, MI

It has been posted for ☒ 3 continous weeks ☐ ___ continuous weeks ___ as ordered by this court.

4-15-89

Chester Gunn
Affiant signature

Date

OJIBWAY ___ County, Michigan.

Subscribed and sworn to before me on ___ Date 4-15-89

Signature: *Loretta Smiley*
Court clerk/Notary public

My commission expires: 1-1-90
Date

AFFIDAVIT OF MAILING

Attach mailing receipt and return receipt here

ATTACH BOTH PS FORM 3806 AND PS FORM 3811

I mailed a copy of the attached summons and

As ordered, on ___ Date 3-18-89

complaint and this order to ___ Name DUDLEY E. LOVELACE

at 900 S. MAPLE, LAKE CITY, MI
Address

The mailing receipt and return receipt are attached at right.

3-18-89

Ruth Darling
Affiant signature

Date

OJIBWAY ___ County, Michigan.

...nd sworn to before me on ___ Date 3-18-89

Signature: *Loretta Smiley*
Court clerk/Notary public

...on expires: 1-1-90
Date

HELPER/SERVER WHO PERFORMED REGISTERED MAILING MUST COMPLETE

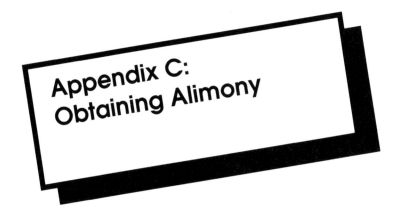

Appendix C: Obtaining Alimony

If you and the defendant have agreed on the payment of periodic alimony, you must take several extra steps described in this appendix. At the beginning of your divorce, you must ask for alimony in paragraph #8c of your Complaint for Divorce (GRP 1),* and show: 1) your need for the alimony 2) the defendant's ability to pay it. If you omit this request, you may not be able to get alimony later.

As an alimony-seeker, you must bring the friend of the court" into your divorce case. The friend of the court is a family court official with a number of duties in divorce cases with minor children. The friend of the court isn't ordinarily involved in cases without minor children. However, the friend of the court must be brought into divorces without minor children whenever alimony is sought. To add the friend of the court to your case, use the following procedures:

Notice to the friend of the court. The friend of the court must receive notice of your divorce by getting copies of all your divorce papers. To do that, make extra copies of the divorce papers (generally three instead of two) and mark the upper left corners of the copies with the notation "FOC." As you file your divorce papers with the clerk, give the extra marked copies to the clerk. The clerk will forward these to the friend of the court.

---

*   As mentioned in "Alimony" on page 11, the divorce papers call alimony by its real name: spousal support.

Information for the friend of the court. Although the divorce papers provide a good deal of information about your marriage, the friend of the court needs more personal and financial information. The friend of the court gets that extra information in the Verified Statement (FOC 23). This paper must be given to the clerk along with your initial divorce papers when you file for divorce. Unlike the other divorce papers, the clerk doesn't place the Verified Statement (FOC 23) in your court file. Instead, the clerk forwards the statement to the friend of the court, without keeping a copy for itself. However, a copy of the Verified Statement (FOC 23) must be included in your service papers and served on the defendant.

Friend of the court fee. You must pay a special fee to cover the cost of the friend of the court's services in your case.* The amount of the fee varies according to the friend of the court's involvement in a divorce:

- $30 in cases with no investigation or mediation by the friend of the court
- $50 in cases mediated by the friend of the court
- $70 in cases where there is an investigation and recommendation by the friend of the court

You will probably owe the minimum $30 fee since neither mediation nor investigation/recommendation should be necessary when alimony is uncontested. The law seems to require payment of the friend of the court at the end of the divorce. But some counties want the fee at the beginning, during filing.

Friend of the court pamphlet. While you're at the clerk's office filing your divorce, ask the clerk for two copies of the friend of the court pamphlet. The pamphlet describes the office of the friend of the court and its role in divorce. Keep one pamphlet for yourself. The other must be served on the defendant with the service papers. After service, list the friend of the court pamphlet in the proof of service as having been served on the defendant.

Because you aren't contesting alimony, the friend of the court probably won't intervene in your divorce. But it could decide to investigate alimony and submit a recommendation to the judge on the issue. If so, you should take the recommendation into account when you prepare the alimony provision in your divorce judgment. Whatever happens, see "Alimony Provisions" in Appendix E for more about providing for either short- or long-term periodic alimony in your judgment.

---

* You may be excused from paying the friend of the court fee if you obtain a fee exemption, as described in Appendix A.

Original - Friend of the Court
1st copy - Plaintiff/Attorney
2nd copy - Defendant/Attorney

CASE NO.

Approved, SCAO

STATE OF MICHIGAN
JUDICIAL CIRCUIT
COUNTY

VERIFIED STATEMENT

1. Mother's last name	First name	Middle name	2. Any other names by which wife is or has been known
			5. Driver license number and state
LOVELACE	DARLENE	ANN	M 650 603 440 886 MICH.

3. Date of birth 5-1-65

4. Social security number 380-16-1010

6. Mailing address and residence address (if different) 121 S. MAIN, LAKE CITY, MI 48800		11. Race WHITE	12. Scars, tattoos, etc.
7. Eye color BLUE	8. Hair color BLONDE	9. Height 5'6"	10. Weight 120	15. Maiden name ALBRIGHT	16. Occupation WAITRESS
13. Home telephone no. 772-0000	14. Work telephone no. 772-0011			18. Gross weekly income $250

17. Business/Employer's name and address 10,000 PANCAKES, 111 M-78, LAKE CITY, MI 48800

19. Has wife applied for or does she receive public assistance? If yes, please specify kind.   20. AFDC and recipient identification numbers
☐ Yes ☒ No

21. Father's last name	First name	Middle name	22. Any other names by which husband is or has been known
			25. Driver license number and state
LOVELACE	DUDLEY	ERNEST	M 649 601 402 701 MICH.

23. Date of birth 6-15-64

24. Social security number 379-10-5567

26. Mailing address and residence address (if different) 900 S. MAPLE, LAKE CITY, MI 48800		31. Race WHITE	32. Scars, tattoos, etc.
27. Eye color BROWN	28. Hair color BLACK	29. Height 6'	30. Weight 170	35. Occupation SALESMAN	37. Gross weekly income $375
33. Home telephone no. 773-3004	34. Work telephone no. 773-0011			

36. Business/Employer's name and address WATERBED WORLD, 1000 SERVICE RD., LAKE CITY, MI 48800

38. Has husband applied for or does he receive public assistance? If yes, please specify kind.   39. AFDC and recipient identification numbers
☐ Yes ☒ No

40. a. Name of Minor Child Involved in Case	b. Birth Date	c. Age	d. Soc. Sec. No.	e. Residential Address

| 41. a. Name of Other Minor Child of Either Party | b. Birth Date | c. Age | d. Soc. Sec. No. | e. Residential Address |
| | | | | |

42. Health care coverage available for each minor child			c. Name of Insurance Co./HMO	d. Policy/Certificate/Contract No.
a. Name of Minor Child	b. Name of Policy Holder			

43. Names and addresses of person(s) other than parties, if any, who may have custody of child(ren) during pendency of this case

• If any of the public assistance information above changes before your judgment is entered, you are required to give the Friend of the Court written notice of the change.

I declare that the statements above are true to the best of my information, knowledge, and belief.

Darlene A. Lovelace
Signature

MCR 3.206(B)

2-28-89
Date
FOC 23 (5/93) **VERIFIED STATEMENT**

Appendix D: Dismissing Your Divorce

If you and your spouse reconcile during the divorce, you may be anxious to dismiss the divorce right away. But this may not always be wise. It takes a lot of work to file a divorce, so why jeopardize all your effort with a hasty dismissal? Wait a while and see if the reconciliation lasts. If it does, go ahead and dismiss your divorce as described below. But if your reconciliation fails, pick up the divorce where you left off and finish it.

At one time, it was possible to let a divorce stay in court for months or even years while the parties attempted reconciliation. These days, courts are under pressure to move cases along quickly, so they won't tolerate much delay. Nevertheless, you probably could let your divorce sit for a few months. Just make sure that your proof of service is on file with the clerk, or else the clerk may dismiss the case for no progress after the 91-day summons expiration period (see "Filing the Proof of Service" on page 68 for more about this danger).

After you decide that your reconciliation is going to last, go ahead and dismiss your divorce. To dismiss your uncontested divorce, fill out the Notice of Dismissal by Plaintiff section of the Dismissal (MC 09). Choose dismissal "without prejudice" because this makes it easier to file another divorce later if your marriage breaks down again. After you prepare the Dismissal (MC 09), file it with the clerk and send a copy to the defendant.

Incidentally, if your fees were suspended at the beginning of the divorce, you must deal with the fees again before you file the Dismissal (MC 09). At that time, the court can order a final fee exemption or require payment of the fees (see Appendix A for more about the fee exemption procedure).

Original - Court
1st copy - Applicant
Other copies - All appearing parties

CASE NO.

Approved, SCAO

STATE OF MICHIGAN
JUDICIAL DISTRICT
JUDICIAL CIRCUIT
COUNTY PROBATE

DISMISSAL

Court telephone no.

Court address

Plaintiff name(s) and address(es)

Defendant name(s) and address(es)

v

Defendant's attorney, bar no., address, and telephone no.

Plaintiff's attorney, bar no., address, and telephone no.

☒ **NOTICE OF DISMISSAL BY PLAINTIFF**   ☐ with   prejudice as to:
                                                       ☒ without

1. Plaintiff/Attorney for plaintiff files this notice of dismissal of this case
   ☒ all defendants.
   ☐ the following defendant(s): _____

2. I certify, under penalty of contempt, that:
   a. This notice is the first dismissal filed by the plaintiff based upon or including the same claim against the defendant.
   b. All costs of filing and service have been paid.
   c. **No answer or motion has been served upon the plaintiff by the defendant** as of the date of this notice.
   d. A copy of this notice has been provided to the appearing defendant/attorney by ☒ mail ☐ personal service.

Darlene A. Lovelace
Plaintiff/Attorney signature

7-1-89
Date

☐ **STIPULATION TO DISMISS**   ☐ with   prejudice as to:
                                          ☐ without

I stipulate to the dismissal of this case
   ☐ all parties.
   ☐ the following parties: _____

_____
Plaintiff/Attorney signature

_____
Date

_____
Defendant/Attorney signature

_____
Date

☐ **ORDER TO DISMISS**   ☐ with   prejudice. Conditions, if any: _____
                                    ☐ without

IT IS ORDERED this case is dismissed

_____
                                                       Bar no.

_____
Judge   MCR 2.504

_____
Date

MC 09 (6/97) **DISMISSAL**

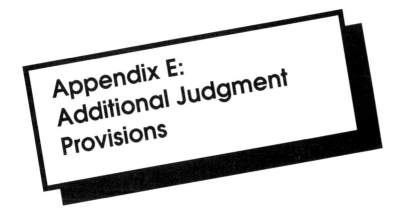

Appendix E:
Additional Judgment
Provisions

The first page of the Judgment of Divorce (GRP 4a) contains standard judgment provisions that should take care of most divorce cases without minor children. But in special cases, these standard provisions might not be enough. Luckily, the judgment form is open-ended allowing you to add extra judgment provisions in the blank space on the Judgment of Divorce (GRP 4e).* If you have a lot of extra judgment provisions that won't fit on just one Judgment of Divorce (GRP 4e), photocopy extras and add them as needed.

The sections below deal with special situations where you might need additional judgment provisions. Sample judgment provisions are also included which you can use or adapt to your case.

Property Division Provisions

Before you can provide for a property division in your judgment, you must do a complete inventory and valuation of your property (see "Can I Get a Fair Property Division?" on page 29 for more about inventorying and valuing property). You and the defendant should also agree to an overall division of your property. If you have a prenuptial agreement dealing with divorce, you will normally use it for the division. Otherwise, you must decide what each of you is to receive. Are you going to divide your property into equal shares, 55-45, 60-40, etc.? After you do all those things, you're ready to begin the actual division of property.

---

*   The missing judgment pages (GRP 4b,c&d) have child custody, parenting time and support provisions for cases with minor children and therefore aren't included in this book.

Dividing Real Property

All real property must be divided specifically in your divorce judgment. This applies equally to real property owned by spouses jointly (joint real property) and real property that a spouse owns alone (solely-owned real property). The provisions below divide joint and solely-owned real property in three ways: 1) trade-off 2) buy-out (by one spouse from the other) 3) sale (to third parties). There are several other ways to divide real property, but they are far too complicated to do by yourself.

If you and your spouse don't own any real property, check the first box in paragraph #5A of the Judgment of Divorce (GRP 4a). If you are property-owners, check the second box and then divide the property in the Judgment of Divorce (GRP 4e). As you divide the real property, include the street address and legal description. Adding the legal description is important because it permits you to use the judgment as a deed substitute if one spouse refuses to sign a deed for the property (see "Transferring Property" on page 89 for more about using a judgment to transfer property). You can find the legal description in a deed, land contract, mortgage, abstract of title or title insurance policy for the property.

Joint Real Property

If you do nothing with your joint real property in your divorce judgment, it automatically converts to tenancy in common ownership. This might be acceptable for a while. As tenants in common, you and the defendant would each get an equal share of the property. If either of you were to die, your share would pass to your heirs/will beneficiaries, not to your ex-spouse, because there aren't rights of survivorship for tenancy in common property.

But in the long run, tenancy in common ownership isn't practical for divorced persons. A tenancy in common is really like a partnership. Both tenants in common have an equal right to possess and use the property, and each has a duty to maintain it. This kind of close-knit arrangement is seldom suitable for ex-spouses.

Consequently, you should divide your joint real property in another way. The provisions below suggest several division options, some of which you may be able to handle yourself.

Trade-Off

If enough property is available, one spouse can trade his/her share of the joint property for an equivalent amount of other property. For example, let's say that spouses jointly own a house worth $50,000 and have $50,000 of miscellaneous property. If the spouses agree to an equal property division, the defendant could trade his/her one-half share of the house for the plaintiff's half-interest in the miscellaneous property. After giving all the miscellaneous property to the defendant elsewhere in the property division, the spouses might use a provision like the one below to give the joint property to the plaintiff:

12. <u>Real Property.</u> Plaintiff is awarded the property located at 121 S. Main, Lake City, Michigan, and described below, free of any claims of defendant:

Lot 2 of Assessor's Plat, Lake City, Ojibway County, Michigan

Plaintiff shall be responsible for any indebtedness against the property and hold defendant harmless from liability for this debt.

Buy-Out

Instead of a trade-off, one spouse could purchase the other's share of the joint real property. The provision below provides for a buy-out of the defendant's share by the plaintiff for cash:

12. <u>Real Property.</u> Plaintiff shall be awarded the property located at 121 S. Main, Lake City, Michigan, and described below, free of any claims of defendant upon the payment of $25,000 to defendant:

Lot 2 of Assessor's Plat, Lake City, Ojibway County, Michigan

Plaintiff shall be responsible for any indebtedness against the property and hold defendant harmless from liability for this debt.

This provision lets the plaintiff buy out the defendant with a single cash payment. If the buyer-spouse can't afford to pay cash, s/he could make installment payments. But to provide for that type of buy-out, one must know about installment sales, how to secure them and their tax consequences. All these things are quite complicated, so seek legal help if you want to provide for a buy-out on an installment basis.

Sale

The sale of joint property to third parties is another way to handle joint property. You can arrange for an immediate sale at the time of your divorce or delay the sale until later. Either way, the sale provision will usually convert the joint property into a tenancy in common until the sale. Then, the provision will typically require: 1) payment of any mortgage or land contract against the property 2) payment of all selling costs (broker's commission, closing costs, etc.) 3) division of any remaining proceeds. A good sale provision should also say who shall possess and maintain the property before the sale. All these things are included in the immediate sale provision below:

12. <u>Real Property.</u> The property located at 121 S. Main, Lake City, Michigan, and described below, shall be owned by plaintiff and defendant as tenants in common:

Lot 2 of Assessor's Plat, Lake City, Ojibway County, Michigan

This property shall be sold as soon as possible at a price and terms the parties shall agree upon. After the property is sold, the proceeds of the sale shall be applied first to satisfy any indebtedness against the property, then against all the costs of sale (including any broker's commission and closing costs). Any remainder shall be divided [equally] between the parties.

Until the closing of the sale, plaintiff shall have sole possession of the property. Plaintiff shall be responsible for any mortgage or land contract payments, taxes, insurance and other expenses of maintaining the property during that time until the day of closing.

An immediate sale is simple and provides for a clean break between the spouses. There are also sound tax reasons for selling real property around the time of a divorce, especially when the property is the former marital home. However, an immediate sale may displace a spouse living at the home.

A delayed sale can solve that problem. It can permit the in-home spouse to live in the former marital home for a while; yet will eventually allow the other spouse to receive his/her share of the property when the delayed sale occurs. The trouble is, a delayed sale is difficult to provide for in a judgment. The events triggering the delayed sale (a date, the remarriage of the in-home spouse, etc.) must be anticipated and carefully described in the provision. The other spouse may want interest on his/her share of the property, and have it protected by a mortgage or other security. Finally, the income tax consequences from a delayed sale can be bad. For all these reasons, if you want a delayed sale, go to a lawyer for help.

Solely-Owned Real Property

If you fail to deal with solely-owned real property in your judgment, the owner-spouse retains ownership of the property free of any claim or interest of the other spouse (in part, that's what paragraph #6 of the Judgment of Divorce (GRP 4a) is about). But you shouldn't leave it at that. Even if you want the owner-spouse to keep his/her solely-owned property (presumably because of a trade-off or buy-out), you should say so in your judgment. When you want another disposition of the property, such as a sale to a third party, you must provide for that as well.

Trade-Off

In this case, the nonowner is trading off his/her "share" in the owner-spouse's solely-owned real property for equivalent property elsewhere in the property division. The owner-spouse keeps ownership of the property:

12. <u>Real Property.</u> Plaintiff is awarded the property located at 121 S. Main, Lake City, Michigan, and described below, free of any claims of defendant:

    Lot 2 of Assessor's Plat, Lake City, Ojibway County, Michigan

    Plaintiff shall be responsible for any indebtedness against the property and hold defendant harmless from liability for this debt.

The owner-spouse buys out the nonowner's "share" in his/her solely-owned real property for cash:*

12. <u>Real Property.</u> Plaintiff shall be awarded the property located at 121 S. Main, Lake City, Michigan, and described below. free of any claims of defendant upon the payment of $25,000 to defendant:

Lot 2 of Assessor's Plat, Lake City, Ojibway County, Michigan

Plaintiff shall be responsible for any indebtedness against the property and hold defendant harmless from liability for this debt.

In this scenario, the solely-owned property must be sold as soon as possible to a third party followed by a division of the proceeds:**

12. <u>Real Property.</u> The property located at 121 S. Main, Lake City, Michigan, and described below, shall be owned by plaintiff and defendant as tenants in common:

Lot 2 of Assessor's Plat, Lake City, Ojibway County, Michigan

This property shall be sold as soon as possible at a price and terms the parties shall agree upon. After the property is sold, the proceeds of the sale shall be applied first to satisfy any indebtedness against the property, then against all the costs of sale (including any broker's commission and closing costs). Any remainder shall be divided [equally] between the parties.

Until the closing of the sale, plaintiff shall have sole possession of the property. Plaintiff shall be responsible for any mortgage or land contract payments, taxes, insurance and other expenses of maintaining the property during that time until the day of closing.

Dividing Personal Property

You may have already divided the bulk of your personal property, such as clothing, household goods, bank accounts and motor vehicles, during or even before your divorce. Courts usually permit informal divisions of personal property because they know that you cannot wait until the end of

---

* As an alternative, you can provide for an installment sale. But as explained above, that is probably too difficult for you to arrange yourself.

** Instead of an immediate sale, you could choose a delayed sale. Yet, as mentioned above, you will probably need legal help to provide for that arrangement.

your divorce to divide essential items. If you have already divided some or all of your personal property that way, confirm the division by checking the first box in paragraph #5B of the Judgment of Divorce (GRP 4a).

On the other hand, you should specifically mention personal property that hasn't yet been transferred to the intended recipient at the time of your final hearing. This avoids confusion about ownership later. For example, if you and the defendant have agreed that the defendant must give you an automobile, a dinette set and a $1,000 bank account, you should say so in your judgment. Check the second box in paragraph #5B of the Judgment of Divorce (GRP 4a), and include the following provision in the Judgment of Divorce (GRP 4e):

12. <u>Personal Property.</u> Plaintiff is awarded the following personal property free of any claims of defendant:

1984 Dodge Aries VIN VL29C4B266259

Five-piece (table and four chairs) Contemporary dinette set

Ojibway State Bank savings account #00012400-001 with a current balance of $1,000

Plaintiff shall be responsible for any indebtedness against this property and hold defendant harmless from liability for this debt.

You can adapt this provision to divide almost any type of personal property. But use it only for the distribution of *important* items of personal property. Don't clutter up your judgment by mentioning every stick of furniture or piece of clothing.

Whenever you use such a provision, include a complete description of the property since this aids transfer of the item later (see "After Your Divorce" on page 89 for more information about transferring property). Describe the property fully and mention any identification numbers (account numbers for financial accounts, vehicle identification numbers ("VINs") for automobiles, hull numbers for boats, etc.), as in the example above.

Dividing Retirement Benefits, Businesses and Other New Property

A divorce property division isn't complete without considering so-called new property (retirement benefits, businesses, etc.). The problem is, new property is often difficult to divide. Unlike a house or an automobile, you can't put retirement benefits on the market, sell them and divide the proceeds (most retirement plans prohibit this kind of sale or transfer even if you could find a buyer). A business can also be hard to liquidate. Some one-person businesses depend on the skill of their owner-operators and may be impossible to sell as going concerns. And even when a small business can be sold, it must often be sold as a piece because few people will buy a share of a small business. Despite these problems, the law has devised ways to divide new property, often without actually distributing it.

Dividing Retirement Benefits

Michigan courts have approved two methods for dividing retirement benefits: 1) trade-off 2) division of payments. In a trade-off, the non-employee-spouse trades off his/her interest in the retirement benefits for a like share of other property. As an example, let's assume that a couple owns an automobile worth $10,000 and the husband has retirement benefits with a present value of $10,000. If the spouses agree to an equal property division, the wife might trade her one-half interest in the retirement benefits for the husband's half-interest in the automobile. Thus, the retirement benefits stay with the husband, but the wife gets the automobile. By this means, the retirement benefits have been divided, but without actually distributing them.

The other method of division—division of payments— results in the actual distribution of retirement benefits to both spouses. With this method, the retirement benefits are divided fractionally between the spouses as payments are made. For example, if the husband is receiving monthly payments, and the parties want an equal division of property, they could assign one-half of the payments to each spouse monthly.

Each of these methods has pluses and minuses. Trade-off is nice because it gives the nonemployee-spouse value immediately, without waiting for the retirement plan to mature (pay benefits). But it requires an estimation of the present value of the retirement plan, which is complicated (see "Can I Get a Fair Property Division?" on page 29 for more about the valuation of retirement plans). Trade-off also places the risk that the employee-spouse will never collect benefits (because of premature death, early retirement, discharge, bankruptcy of the employer, etc.) on the employee-spouse alone. If the employee-spouse never gets the benefits, s/he has traded off other property for nothing. And finally, a trade-off may not be possible if the value of the retirement benefits is great and there is no other property that can be traded for them.

It's simpler to just divide the retirement benefits. Unlike a trade-off, you normally won't have to estimate the total value of the benefits, since you're dividing the payments, not the total benefits package. This avoids making a difficult present value calculation. Dividing payments also places the risks associated with the retirement benefits on both spouses. If the retirement plan fails, both spouses share the loss; if benefits increase in the future, each spouse shares in the gain.

But unless the retirement plan is mature, dividing payments often won't give the nonemployee-spouse any property immediately after the divorce. What's more, a division of payments order is difficult to provide for in a divorce judgment. You must use precise language or it won't be legally effective. For this reason, if you want to divide retirement benefits in your divorce yourself, you will have to use the trade-off method. To do that, simply check the first box in paragraph #8 of your Judgment of Divorce (GRP 4a), and then give or get equivalent property elsewhere in the property division. If you want to use the division of payments method, see a lawyer.

Individual retirement arrangements (IRAs), which are individual retirement plans, can be divided in several ways, including: 1) transfer from the owner-spouse to the other spouse 2) trade-off 3) withdrawal and division of the proceeds.

To transfer an IRA, describe the account and provide for transfer in a judgment provision, like the bank account example above. This kind of divorce-related transfer isn't considered a withdrawal, so no tax or early withdrawal penalty is imposed. But tax and an early withdrawal penalty may be due if the new owner of the account withdraws money from it prematurely. If you want to trade off an IRA for other property, make sure that you have checked the first box in paragraph #8 of your Judgment of Divorce (GRP 4a), and give the nonowner-spouse equivalent property elsewhere in the judgment. You can also withdraw the money in an IRA and divide it. But if the IRA owner is younger than $59\frac{1}{2}$, that's a premature withdrawal and a penalty will be imposed.

Keogh (HR-10) plans are another type of individual retirement plan. Like IRAs, they can be transferred, traded off or withdrawn and divided. But transferring or withdrawing Keoghs can have bad tax consequences, leaving trade-off as the best method of division in most cases.

Dividing Businesses and Other New Property

Business interests can be transferred between spouses or liquidated and divided. In many cases, trade-off is the best method of division. To trade off a business, create a judgment provision like the one below, assigning the business to the business-owner, and then give the nonbusiness-owner equivalent property elsewhere in the property division.

12. <u>Personal Property.</u> Defendant is awarded all the assets, including inventory, supplies, fixtures, equipment, accounts and goodwill, in the House of Waterbeds, Lake City, Michigan, free of any claims of plaintiff. Defendant shall hold plaintiff harmless from any liability in connection with this business.

Division of Debts

As you end your marriage, who is responsible for debts you leave behind? If you do nothing, the following general rules govern liability for your sole debts (debts incurred by a spouse alone) and joint debts (debts taken on by spouses together):

Sole debt. The spouse who incurred the debt (debtor-spouse) remains liable for it after the divorce. The nondebtor-spouse won't be liable for the debt unless one of the following exceptions applies:

¶ *Necessaries.* Necessaries are things such as food, clothing, shelter, health care, etc., necessary for survival. According to Michigan law, the nondebtor-spouse may be liable for the costs of family necessaries obtained by the debtor-spouse.

¶ *Agency.* If the nondebtor-spouse gave the debtor-spouse the authority, as an agent, to incur debts on his/her behalf, the nondebtor-spouse is liable for the debts. Even without such express authority, similar liability can be created when the nondebtor-spouse: 1) leads creditors to believe that the debtor-spouse can incur debts on his/her behalf 2) approves any debts incurred by the debtor-spouse.

Joint debt. Because both spouses incurred joint debts, each remains liable for these after the divorce.

By dividing debts in your divorce judgment, you can modify this liability to an extent. A debt provision can shift the liability for a sole debt from the debtor-spouse to the other spouse. It could also have one spouse assume liability for a joint debt or a sole debt for which both spouses are liable under one of the exceptions described above.

Not all debts are good candidates for division. Educational and personal loans are better left with those incurring them, since they have a bigger incentive to pay them. Likewise, debts secured by property (mortgages, land contracts and other liens) are customarily transferred to the recipients of the secured property. (For this reason, all the sample property division provisions in this appendix transfer secured debts along with the property securing them.) On the other hand, general unsecured debts, such as credit card or charge account debts, are good choices for division.

Whatever you decide, any debt provision you insert in your judgment must describe the debt and say who is responsible for paying it, as in the following provision:

12. <u>Debts.</u> Defendant is responsible for, and must hold plaintiff harmless from, the following debts:

Lake City Department Store charge account #22224445 with a current balance of $540

Mastercredit account #5215 0200 3400 6529 with a current balance of $1,233.33

Debt Division and Creditors

Although you and the defendant can rearrange debts in your judgment, your arrangements won't affect the rights of the creditors holding the debts. Your creditors will have the same rights after your divorce as they had before.*

Example: A couple got a joint car loan from a bank (creditor). In their divorce, the wife got the car and the loan was assigned to her in the

---

* A creditor can agree to release a spouse from liability for a joint debt. In that case, the released spouse would no longer be liable to the creditor for the debt. Nevertheless, most creditors won't consent to such releases because they prefer to have two debtors rather than one.

judgment. She falls behind on the car payments. The bank could sue the husband because the debt division didn't affect his liability to the bank.

If a debt division doesn't change creditors' rights, why go to the trouble of dividing debts in your divorce judgment? The advantage to debt division is that it provides a legal claim, known as indemnity, against the spouse assuming the debt. The indemnity can then be used as a defense or a direct claim.

> **Glossary**
>
> *Indemnity*–legal claim making someone else answerable for your obligation to a third person.

Example: A couple gets a joint car loan from a bank (creditor). In their divorce, the wife gets the car and agrees to pay the loan off in a debt division provision. After she falls behind in car payments, the bank sues both spouses. The husband could cite the indemnity from the debt division and shift liability to the wife. Had the bank sued the husband alone, he could add the wife to the case and raise the indemnity against her.

Alimony Provisions

Every divorce judgment must deal with alimony* and settle the issue for *both* spouses by either: 1) waiving (surrendering) 2) reserving 3) or granting alimony.

When you want to waive alimony for you or the defendant, indicate in paragraph #4 of your Judgment of Divorce (GRP 4a) that alimony is "not granted for" that particular party. By making that choice, you permanently waive alimony for the party whose box you have checked, and s/he won't be permitted to seek alimony later.

If you want to leave the issue of alimony open for a party, check the box indicating that alimony is "reserved for" that party. You cannot reserve alimony merely because you find the issue of alimony bothersome and don't want to deal with it during your divorce. To reserve alimony, you must have a good reason for the reservation, such as: 1) there is only limited jurisdiction in the case (see "Can I Get a Divorce in Michigan?" on page 24 about why limited jurisdiction isn't enough for alimony) 2) the payer is elusive or has disappeared and you cannot determine his/her ability to pay alimony 3) the would-be recipient of the alimony is making a personal or career change and isn't sure of his/her financial needs now. When alimony is reserved for a party, s/he can come back to court later and ask for alimony. At that time, the court will decide whether it should be paid.

If you and the defendant have agreed on some type of alimony, check the box that says alimony is "granted elsewhere in this judgment for" the recipient. You must then include an alimony provision in your Judgment of Divorce (GRP 4e) (see below for sample alimony provisions).

---

*   In the judgment, alimony is called by its real name: spousal support.

As you're dealing with alimony in your judgment, make sure that you settle it for both of you in one of the three ways described above. If you fail to settle alimony for a party, the failure automatically reserves alimony for that party, allowing him/her to seek it later.

The alimony provisions below are for short- and long-term periodic alimony. Both provisions make the alimony subject to several conditions. You can omit any of these or add others. But keep in mind that the death-of-the-recipient condition is necessary to qualify the payments as alimony for federal tax purposes. Without that condition, the payments won't be deductible by the payer. Because these are periodic alimony provisions, they're always subject to post-divorce modification if there is a change in the parties' circumstances.

Short-Term Alimony

12. <u>Spousal Support.</u> Defendant shall pay $50 per week to plaintiff through the office of the friend of the court as periodic spousal support. Spousal support shall be modifiable. Payment of this support shall begin on September 7, 1989, and end immediately on the happening of any of the following events:

(a) [September 7, 1991]

(b) death of plaintiff

(c) death of defendant

(d) remarriage of plaintiff

(e) cohabitation by plaintiff with a member of the opposite sex

After plaintiff's spousal support ends, it shall be forever barred to her.

Long-Term Alimony

12. <u>Spousal Support.</u> Defendant shall pay $50 per week to plaintiff through the office of the friend of the court as periodic spousal support. Spousal support shall be modifiable. Payment of this support shall begin on September 7, 1989, and end immediately on the happening of any of the following events:

(a) death of plaintiff

(b) death of defendant

(c) remarriage of plaintiff

(d) cohabitation by plaintiff with a member of the opposite sex

After plaintiff's spousal support ends, it shall be forever barred to her.

When you provide for alimony, you must add several provisions to your judgment. These are standard provisions required whenever support, such as alimony, is ordered. You can add these extra provisions to your judgment immediately below the alimony provision in the Judgment of Divorce (GRP 4e):

13. <u>Future Modification of Support.</u>   Except as otherwise provided in section 3 of the Support and Parenting time Enforcement Act, Act No. 295 of the Public Acts of 1982, being section 552.603 of the Michigan Compiled Laws, a support order that is part of a judgment or is an order in a domestic relation matter as that term is defined in section 31 of the Friend of the Court Act, Act. No. 294 of the Public Acts of 1982, being section 552.531 of the Michigan Compiled Laws, is a judgment on and after the date each support payment is due, with the full force, effect, and attributes of a judgment of this state, and is not, on and after the date it is due, subject to retroactive modification. A surcharge of 8% annually will be added to support payments that are past due as of January 1 and July 1 of each year as provided in MCL 552.603a.

14. <u>Personal Information.</u> The parties shall notify the friend of the court in writing of changes in their addresses no later than 21 days after a change. They shall also promptly notify the friend of the court of changes in their sources of income, occupational or driver's licenses and health care coverage.

    <u>Plaintiff's personal information:</u>

    Residence address: [121 S. Main, Lake City, MI, 48800]
    Social security number: [380-16-1010]
    Source of income name: [10,000 Pancakes]
    Source of income address: [111 M-78, Lake City, MI, 48800]
    Occupational license type and number: [None]
    Driver's license number: [M 650 603 440 886 Mich.]
    Health care coverage: [Lake City Health Alliance, contract #1669789] covering [Darlene A. Lovelace DOB: 5-1-65]

    <u>Defendant's personal information:</u>

    Residence address: [900 S. Maple, Lake City, MI, 48800]
    Social security number: [379-10-5567]
    Source of income name: [Waterbed World]
    Employer's address: [1000 Service Rd., Lake City, MI, 48800]
    Occupational license type and number: [None]
    Driver's license number: [M 649 601 402 701 Mich.]
    Health care coverage: [Lakeview HMO, contract #226-8978-24] covering [Dudley E. Lovelace DOB: 6-15-64]

Choosing an Alimony Payment Method

When you provide for alimony, you must also arrange for a method of payment. You have several payment options: 1) immediate income withholding 2) payment to the friend of the court 3) direct payment to the alimony recipient.

These days, immediate income withholding is the standard method of paying all kinds of support, so most alimony is paid this way. When alimony is paid by immediate income withholding, money is withheld from the payer's source of income (typically an employer), and sent to the friend of the court for transfer to the recipient.

To obtain immediate income withholding, you must use an Income Withholding Order (FOC 5) and add several paragraphs to your Judgment of Divorce (GRP 4). Before the final hearing, prepare the Income Withholding Order (FOC 5) as shown in the sample form at the end of this appendix. Then add the following paragraphs to your Judgment of Divorce (GRP 4e), just below the other alimony provisions described above:

15. <u>Income Withholding.</u> Income withholding shall continue or be implemented immediately upon entry of this judgment.

16. <u>Service Fees.</u> The payer of support shall pay to the office of the friend of the court a service fee of $2.00 per month, payable semi-annually on January 2 and July 2 of each year. In addition, every person required to make payments of support or maintenance through the office of the friend of the court shall pay $1.25 per month for every or portion of a month that support or maintenance is required to be paid to cover the cost of services provided by the office of the friend of the court which are not reimbursed under title IV-D.

Immediate income withholding is popular with alimony recipients and the courts because it makes alimony easy to collect. By the same token, some alimony payers dislike it because it creates more paperwork for their employers. They may want to avoid immediate income withholding and set up a different method of payment.

If alimony isn't immediately withheld, the payer can pay it to the friend of the court or directly to the recipient. Alimony payers may like payment to the recipient because it's informal with less paperwork. But recipients usually prefer payment to the friend of the court as this offers better collection, record-keeping and enforcement of the alimony.

There are two ways to avoid immediate income withholding and choose another payment method. The alimony payer and recipient can agree to the avoidance by signing an agreement form. You can also avoid immediate income withholding without the consent of the other party for "good cause." The court must approve the arrangement in either case.

You need two forms to avoid immediate income withholding by agreement: 1) Agreement Suspending Immediate Income Withholding (FOC 63) 2) Order Suspending Immediate Income Withholding (FOC 64). Prepare these papers before the final hearing, when you do your other final divorce papers. Omit the Income Withholding Order (FOC 5) described above since you're not having income withheld.

Describe your alternate alimony payment method in the space in paragraph #2 of the Agreement Suspending Immediate Income Withholding (FOC 63). If you want payment to the friend of the court, simply say that in paragraph #2. Your alimony provision itself, if it resembles the short- and long-term sample provisions above, also provides for payment through the friend of the court. But add this provision below the other alimony paragraphs:

15. <u>Service Fees.</u>   The payer of support shall pay to the office of the friend of the court a service fee of $2.00 per month, payable semi-annually on January 2 and July 2 of each year. In addition, every person required to make payments of support or maintenance through the office of the friend of the court shall pay $1.25 per month for every or portion of a month that support or maintenance is required to be paid to cover the cost of services provided by the office of the friend of the court which are not reimbursed under title IV-D.

If you've agreed to direct payment to the alimony recipient, state that in the space in paragraph #2 of the Agreement Suspending Immediate Income Withholding (FOC 63). You must also amend your alimony provision, removing payment of the spousal support "through the office of the friend of the court."

During the final hearing, give the Agreement Suspending Immediate Income Withholding (FOC 63) and Order Suspending Immediate Income Withholding (FOC 64) to the judge. Tell the judge that you want to avoid immediate income withholding and explain the alternate payment method you want.

If the judge approves your arrangement, s/he will sign the Order Suspending Immediate Income Withholding (FOC 64). File that order and the Agreement Suspending Immediate Income Withholding (FOC 63) with the clerk (with copies for the friend of the court) when you file the Judgment of Divorce (GRP 4). Afterward, send copies of the two papers to the defendant along with the judgment, and list them in the Proof of Mailing (MC 302).

To avoid immediate income withholding for good cause without the consent of the other party, prepare your judgment and other final divorce papers as described above in this section. But omit the Agreement Suspending Immediate Income Withholding (FOC 63).

Describe the good cause for avoiding immediate income withholding in the space in paragraph #2 of the Order Suspending Immediate Income Withholding (FOC 64). If you want payment through the friend of the court, make sure your alimony provision provides for that method of payment, as the sample provisions do. Also, include this provision below the other alimony paragraphs:

15. <u>Service Fees.</u>   The payer of support shall pay to the office of the friend of the court a service fee of $2.00 per month, payable semi-annually on January 2 and July 2 of each year. In addition, every person required to make payments of support or maintenance through the office of the friend of the court shall pay $1.25 per month for every or portion of a month that support or maintenance is required to be paid to cover the cost of services provided by the office of the friend of the court which are not reimbursed under title IV-D.

For direct payment to the recipient, you must amend your alimony provision, substituting payment directly to the recipient instead of payment "through the office of the friend of the court."

During the final hearing, tell the judge that you want to avoid immediate income withholding. Describe the good cause for the avoidance and the alternate payment method you want. If the payer has been paying alimony, you must also show that s/he has a good payment record.

If the judge approves your arrangement, s/he will sign the Order Suspending Immediate Income Withholding (FOC 64). File the order (and a friend of the court copy) when you file the Judgment of Divorce (GRP 4). Afterward, send a copy of the order to the defendant along with the judgment, and list it in the Proof of Mailing (MC 302).

Approved, SCAO

STATE OF MICHIGAN JUDICIAL CIRCUIT COUNTY	Original - Court 1st copy - Friend of the Court	2nd copy - Plaintiff 3rd copy - Defendant Additional copies to all sources of income

Friend of the Court address

INCOME WITHHOLDING ORDER
☒ Court ordered   ☐ Consent

CASE NO.

Plaintiff's name and address

Court telephone no.

v

Defendant's name and address

Regarding: **DUDLEY E. LOVELACE**
Payer
379-10-5567
Social security number

Date of order: **5-7-89**

Judge: **LESTER TUBBS**

1. The court finds that the above payer owes current support, statutory fees, and/or arrearages in the above case, and notice has been given as required by law.

2. Income is defined as: commissions, earnings, salaries, wages, and other income due now or in the future from an employer and successor employers; any payment due now or in the future from a profit-sharing plan, pension plan, insurance contract, annuity, unemployment compensation, supplemental unemployment benefits, and worker's compensation; any amount of money due the payer under a support order as a debt of any other individual, partnership, association, private or public corporation, the United States or any Federal agency, any state or political subdivision of any state, or any other legal entity indebted to the payer.

IT IS ORDERED:

3. The source of income shall withhold payer's income as specified in the attached notice of income withholding and in any subsequent notices.

4. The friend of the court shall be appointed receiver to receive, take possession, cash, and disburse these funds for the purpose of collecting support, statutory fees, and the payment of all arrearages.

5. Any income withheld under this order shall be paid to the friend of the court within 3 days after the date of withholding.

6. If the payer's existing support order is modified by an order of the court, the office of the friend of the court shall send a notice of modification to the source of income by ordinary mail. The amount assigned or withheld shall be changed to conform with the court modification within 7 days after receipt of the notice of modification.

Darlene A. Lovelace
Signature of preparer

☐ I consent to the terms of this order.
Payer's signature

Lester Tubbs
Judge   Bar no.

CERTIFICATE OF MAILING

I certify that on this date I mailed a copy of this order to the parties and sources of income by ordinary mail addressed to the last known addresses.

Date _____

FOC 5 (3/96) **INCOME WITHHOLDING ORDER**

Signature _____

MCL 552.601 et seq.; MSA 25.164(1) et seq.

Approved, SCAO

STATE OF MICHIGAN
JUDICIAL CIRCUIT
COUNTY

Friend of the Court address

AGREEMENT SUSPENDING
IMMEDIATE INCOME WITHHOLDING

Original - Court
2nd copy - Friend of the Court
3rd copy - Plaintiff
4th copy - Defendant

CASE NO.

Plaintiff's name, address, and social security no.

Court telephone no.

v

Defendant's name, address, and social security no.

NOTE: MCL 552.604(3); MSA 25.164(4)(3) requires that all new and modified support orders after December 31, 1990 include a provision for immediate income withholding and that income withholding take effect immediately unless the parties enter into a written agreement that the income withholding order shall not take effect immediately.

We understand that by law an order of income withholding in a support order shall take effect. agree to the following:

DESCRIBE ALTERNATE METHOD OF PAYMENT

1. The order of income withholding shall not take effect immediately.

2. An alternative payment arrangement shall be made as follows:

THE DEFENDANT SHALL PAY THE SUPPORT THROUGH THE OFFICE OF THE FRIEND OF THE COURT

3. Both the payer and the recipient of support shall keep the friend of the court informed of the following:
   a. the name and address of his/her current source of income;
   b. any health care coverage that is available to him/her as a benefit of employment or that is maintained by him/her; the name of the insurance company, health care organization, or health maintenance organization; the policy, certificate or contract number; and the name(s) and birth date(s) of the person(s) for whose benefit s/he maintains health care coverage under the policy, certificate, or contract; and
   c. his/her current residence and mailing address.

4. We further understand that proceedings to implement income withholding shall commence if the payer of support falls one month behind in his/her support payments.

5. We recognize that the court may order withholding of income to take effect immediately for cause or at the request of the payer.

5-5-89
Date

Darlene A. Lovelace
Plaintiff's signature

5-5-89
Date

Dudley Lovelace
Defendant's signature

FOC 63 (3/93) AGREEMENT SUSPENDING IMMEDIATE INCOME WITHHOLDING

MCL 552.604; MSA 25.164(4)

Original · Court
1st copy · Friend of the Court
2nd copy · Plaintiff
3rd copy · Defendant

Approved, SCAO		CASE NO.
STATE OF MICHIGAN JUDICIAL CIRCUIT COUNTY	ORDER SUSPENDING IMMEDIATE INCOME WITHHOLDING	Court telephone no.

Friend of the Court address

Plaintiff's name, address, and social security no

v

Defendant's name, address, and social security no

Date of hearing: **5-7-89**　　　　Judge: **LESTER TUBBS**　　　　Bar no.

1. Date of hearing: **5-7-89**
2. THE COURT FINDS:
   ☒ There is good cause for the order of income withholding not to take effect immediately as follows:
   a. It is in the best interest of the child for immediate income withholding not to take effect for the following stated reasons:

   THE DEFENDANT IS SELF-EMPLOYED WITH AN IRREGULAR INCOME SO IMMEDIATE INCOME WITHHOLDING IS NOT FEASIBLE.

[handwritten cloud annotation: CHECK THIS BOX AND GIVE REASONS IF YOU ARE AVOIDING IMMEDIATE INCOME WITHHOLDING FOR "GOOD CAUSE" WITHOUT CONSENT OF DEFENDANT]

   ... support has been provided.
   ... the friend of the court in writing of any change in:
   b. ... income;
   c. ... as a benefit of employment or that is maintained by him/her, ...ization, or health maintenance organization; the policy, ...h dates of the persons for whose benefit s/he maintains ... contract; and
   ... 21 days of the change.

   ... has been reviewed and entered in the record as follows:
   ... ct immediately.

   ☐ The parties ...
   a. The order of income withholding ...
   b. An alternative payment arrangement has been agreed upon (attached).
   ... the payer and the recipient of support will notify the friend of the court in writing of any change in:
   c. ...ame and ... ross of his/her current source of income;
      ... able to him/her as a benefit of employment or that is maintained by him/her, ...alth care organization, or health maintenance organization; the policy,
      2) ...ames and birth dates of the persons for whose benefit s/he maintains
      ...ificate, or contract; and
      3) ...s within 21 days of the change.

[handwritten cloud annotation: OR CHECK THIS BOX IF YOU ARE AVOIDING IMMEDIATE INCOME WITHHOLDING BY AGREEMENT]

   IT IS ORDE...
3. Income wi...
4. Income with...　　　　...ount of arrearage is reached, as specified in law.

5-7-89
Date

Lester Tubbs (signature)
Judge

MCL 552.511; MSA 25.176(11),
MCL 552.604; MSA 25.164(4),
MCL 552.607; MSA 25.164(7)

FOC 64 (6/94) ORDER SUSPENDING IMMEDIATE INCOME WITHHOLDING

Forms

Original - Court
1st copy - Defendant
2nd copy - Plaintiff
3rd copy - Return

STATE OF MICHIGAN JUDICIAL DISTRICT JUDICIAL CIRCUIT	SUMMONS AND COMPLAINT	CASE NO.

Court address | Court telephone no.

Plaintiff name(s), address(es), and telephone no(s).	v	Defendant name(s), address(es), and telephone no(s).
Plaintiff attorney, bar no., address, and telephone no.		

NOTICE TO THE DEFENDANT: In the name of the people of the State of Michigan you are notified:

1. You are being sued.
2. YOU HAVE 21 DAYS after receiving this summons to file an answer with the court and serve a copy on the other party or to take other lawful action (28 days if you were served by mail or you were served outside this state).
3. If you do not answer or take other action within the time allowed, judgment may be entered against you for the relief demanded in the complaint.

Issued	This summons expires	Court clerk

*This summons is invalid unless served on or before its expiration date.

☐ There is no other pending or resolved civil action arising out of the same transaction or occurrence as alleged in the complaint/

☐ A civil action between these parties or other parties arising out of the transaction or occurrence alleged in the complaint has been previously filed in_____ Court.

☐ There is no other pending or resolved action within the jurisdiction of the family division of circuit court involving the family or family members of the parties.

☐ An action within the jurisdiction of the family division of the circuit court involving the family or family members of the parties has been previously filed in _____ Court.

The docket number and assigned judge of the civil/domestic relations action are:

Docket no.	Judge	Bar no.

The civil/domestic relations action ☐ remains ☐ is no longer pending.

VENUE	
Plaintiff(s) residence (include city, township, or village)	Defendant(s) residence (include city, township, or village)
Place where action arose or business conducted	

I declare that the complaint information above and attached is true to the best of my information, knowledge, and belief.

_____   _____
Date   Signature of attorney/plaintiff

COMPLAINT IS STATED ON ATTACHED PAGES. EXHIBITS ARE ATTACHED IF REQUIRED BY COURT RULE.

If you require special accommodations to use the court because of disabilities, please contact the court immediately to make arrangements.

MC 01 (11/97) **SUMMONS AND COMPLAINT**   MCR 2.102(B)(11), MCR 2.104, MCR 2.107, MCR 2.113(C)(2)(a), (b), MCR 3.206(A)

	SUMMONS AND COMPLAINT
PROOF OF SERVICE	Case No.

TO PROCESS SERVER: You are to serve the summons and complaint not later than 91 days from the date of filing. You must make and file your return with the court clerk. If you are unable to complete service you must return this original and all copies to the court clerk.

CERTIFICATE / AFFIDAVIT OF SERVICE / NON-SERVICE

☐ **OFFICER CERTIFICATE**	**OR**	☐ **AFFIDAVIT OF PROCESS SERVER**
I certify that I am a sheriff, deputy sheriff, bailiff, appointed court officer, or attorney for a party [MCR 2.104(A)(2)], and that: (notary not required)		Being first duly sworn, I state that I am a legally competent adult who is not a party or an officer of a corporate party, and that: (notary required)

☐ I served personally a copy of the summons and complaint,
☐ I served by registered or certified mail (copy of return receipt attached)   a copy of the summons and complaint,

together with _____ on the defendant(s):
Attachment

Defendant's name	Complete address(es) of service	Day, date, time

☐ After diligent search and inquiry, I have been unable to find and serve the following defendant(s):

_____

I have made the following efforts in attempting to serve process: _____

_____

☐ I have personally attempted to serve the summons and complaint, together with _____
Attachment

_____ on _____
Name

at _____ and have been unable to complete service because
Address

the address was incorrect at the time of filing.

Service fee	Miles traveled	Mileage fee	Total fee	Signature
$		$	$	
				Title

Subscribed and sworn to before me on _____ , _____ County, Michigan.
Date

My commission expires: _____ Signature: _____
Date   Deputy court clerk/Notary public

ACKNOWLEDGMENT OF SERVICE

I acknowledge that I have received service of the summons and complaint, together with _____
Attachment

_____ on _____
Day, date, time

_____ on behalf of _____
Signature

MCR 2.105

STATE OF MICHIGAN JUDICIAL CIRCUIT - FAMILY DIVISION COUNTY	COMPLAINT FOR DIVORCE	CASE NO.

Court address   Court telephone no.

Plaintiff □ husband □ wife	v	Defendant
Plaintiff's name before marriage		Defendant's name before marriage

SUMMONS AND COMPLAINT (MC 01) must be completed and attached.

1. Plaintiff's residence: at least   □ 180 days in Michigan   immediately before filing of this complaint.
                               □ 10 days in this county
                                     and/or

    Defendant's residence: at least   □ 180 days in Michigan   immediately before filing of this complaint.
                               □ 10 days in this county

2. Marriage: _____   _____
            Date   Place

3. The parties stopped living together as husband and wife on or about _____ .

4. There has been a breakdown of the marriage relationship to the extent that the objects of matrimony have been destroyed and there remains no reasonable likelihood that the marriage can be preserved.

5. There are no minor children of the parties or born during the marriage.

6. The wife □ is not □ is pregnant, and the estimated date of birth is _____ .

7. There □ is □ is no property to be divided.

8. I request a judgment of divorce, and:

   a. property   □ award to each party the property in his/her possession
                  □ divide

□ b. change wife's last name to _____ .

□ c. spousal support for: □ plaintiff □ defendant

     plaintiff/defendant earns _____ weekly at _____ and needs the support

     plaintiff/defendant earns _____ weekly at _____ and can provide the support

□ d. other: Specify

_____   _____
Date   Plaintiff signature

STATE OF MICHIGAN JUDICIAL CIRCUIT - FAMILY DIVISION COUNTY	DEFAULT Application, Nonmilitary Affidavit and Entry	CASE NO.

Court address   Court telephone no.

Plaintiff's name, address and social security no.

Plaintiff's attorney, bar no., address and telephone no.

V

Defendant's name, address and social security no.

Defendant's attorney, bar no., address and telephone no.

APPLICATION AND NONMILITARY AFFIDAVIT

I request the clerk to enter the default of the defendant for failure to appear, plead or otherwise defend as provided by law. In support of this request, I state:

1. As shown by the proof of service on file, the defendant was served with a summons and complaint on _____ , which is more than 21 days ago (28 days if served by mail or out of state).

2. The defendant is not an infant, incompetent person or in the military service.

_____
Date

_____
Plaintiff signature

Subscribed and sworn to before me on   _____

_____
Notary Public

_____ County, Michigan

My commission expires: _____

ENTRY

The default of the defendant is entered for failure to appear, plead or otherwise defend.

_____
Date

_____
Court clerk

GRP 2   (2/98)   **DEFAULT, Application, Nonmilitary Affidavit and Entry**

STATE OF MICHIGAN JUDICIAL CIRCUIT - FAMILY DIVISION COUNTY	NOTICE OF ENTRY OF DEFAULT AND REQUEST FOR DEFAULT JUDGMENT OF DIVORCE	CASE NO.

Court address _____ Court telephone no. _____

Plaintiff's name, address and social security no.		Defendant's name, address and social security no.
	V	
Plaintiff's attorney, bar no., address and telephone no.		Defendant's attorney, bar no., address and telephone no.

NOTICE

TO THE DEFENDANT:

1. Your default was entered on _____ , as shown by the attached Default.

2. I will be requesting a default Judgment of Divorce and a hearing on that request is scheduled for _____
   at _____ in the courtroom of the judge in this case.

3. At the hearing, the judge may enter a Judgment of Divorce granting the relief I requested in my Complaint for Divorce and/or grant other relief.

_____   _____
Date   Plaintiff signature

PROOF OF MAILING

On the date below, I sent copies of this notice and the Default entered in this case to the defendant, at his/her address in the caption above, by ordinary first-class mail.

I declare that the statement above is true to the best of my information, knowledge and belief.

_____   _____
Date   Plaintiff signature

GRP 3   (2/98)   **NOTICE OF ENTRY OF DEFAULT AND REQUEST FOR DEFAULT JUDGMENT OF DIVORCE**

STATE OF MICHIGAN JUDICIAL CIRCUIT - FAMILY DIVISION **COUNTY**	**JUDGMENT OF DIVORCE** Page 1 of pages	**CASE NO.**

Court address   Court telephone no.

Plaintiff's name, address and social security no.	V	Defendant's name, address and social security no.
Plaintiff's attorney, bar no., address and telephone no.		Defendant's attorney, bar no., address and telephone no.

☐ After trial   ☐ Default   ☐ Consent

Date of hearing: _____   Judge: _____

IT IS ORDERED:

1. **DIVORCE:** The parties are divorced.

2. **MINOR CHILDREN:** There ☐ are / ☐ are not children under 18 of the parties or born during this marriage.

   (Custody, parenting time, support and/or other required provisions are attached.)

3. **NAME CHANGE:** Wife's last name is changed to _____.

4. **SPOUSAL SUPPORT:** Spousal support is
   - ☐ not granted for   ☐ wife.   ☐ husband.
   - ☐ reserved for   ☐ wife.   ☐ husband.
   - ☐ granted elsewhere in this judgment for   ☐ wife.   ☐ husband.

5. **PROPERTY DIVISION:**

   A. **REAL PROPERTY:** (Land and buildings)
   - ☐ The parties do not own any real property.
   - ☐ Real property is divided elsewhere in this judgment.

   All real property owned by the parties in joint tenancy or tenancy by the entirety is converted to tenancy in common, unless this judgment provides otherwise.

   B. **PERSONAL PROPERTY:** (All other property)
   - ☐ Each party is awarded the personal property in his or her possession.
   - ☐ Personal property is divided elsewhere in this judgment.

6. **STATUTORY RIGHTS:** All interests of the parties in the property of the other, now owned or later acquired, under MCL 700.281-700.292, are extinguished, including those known as dower under MCL 558.1-558.29.

7. **BENEFICIARY RIGHTS:** The rights each party has to the proceeds or policies or contracts of life insurance, endowments, or annuities upon the life of the other as a named beneficiary or by assignment during or in anticipation of marriage, are ☐ extinguished.   ☐ provided for elsewhere in this judgment.

8. **RETIREMENT BENEFITS:** Any rights of either party in any pension, annuity or retirement plan benefit of the other, whether vested or unvested, accumulated or contingent, are ☐ extinguished.   ☐ provided for elsewhere in this judgment.

9. **DOCUMENTATION:** Each party shall promptly and properly execute and deliver to the other documents to carry out the terms of this judgment. A certified copy of this judgment may be recorded with the register of deeds in any county of this state where property may be located.

10. **PREVIOUS ORDERS:** Except as otherwise provided, any nonfinal orders or injunctions entered in this action are terminated.

11. **EFFECTIVE DATE OF JUDGMENT:** This judgment shall become effective immediately after it is signed and filed with the clerk of this court.

STATE OF MICHIGAN JUDICIAL CIRCUIT - FAMILY DIVISION **COUNTY**	**JUDGMENT OF DIVORCE** **Final of** **pages**	**CASE NO.**

Plaintiff	V	Defendant

IT IS FURTHER ORDERED:

Date	Judge

Testimony

1) My name is [full name] , my address is [address], and I am the plaintiff in this case.

2) I was married to the defendant on _____ at _____ by a person authorized to
perform marriages.
Date and place of marriage

3) Before the marriage, my/[my wife's] name was _____ .
Wife's former name

4) I filed my complaint for divorce on _____ . Before I filed the complaint, I had resided in Michigan since
Filing date
_____ and in this county since _____ .
State residency   County residency

5) As I said in my complaint, there has been a breakdown in our marriage relationship to the extent the objects of matrimony
have been destroyed because _____and there remains no
Brief facts to support grounds
reasonable likelihood that our marriage can be preserved because _____ .
Brief facts to support grounds

6) The defendant and I have no minor children, and I/[my wife] am not now pregnant.

7) I am working at_____ and am able to support myself.
Source of support

8) We own some _____ that we have split between us. We have also agreed that
General description of personal property
the defendant is to give me_____ and I will pay off the debt on it.
Specific items of personal property transferred in judgment

9) We also own_____worth around_____ .
Description of any real property   Value
We have agreed to _____ .
Manner of division

10) I would like my former name of _____ back.
Wife's name change

11) My court fees were suspended when I filed this divorce. Since then, _____ .
Current financial condition

12) Does the court have any questions?

STATE OF MICHIGAN **JUDICIAL DISTRICT** **JUDICIAL CIRCUIT**	**PROOF OF MAILING**	CASE NO.

Court address _____ Court telephone no.

Plaintiff(s)		Defendant(s)
	v	

On the date below I sent by first class mail a copy of _____

to: | Names and addresses

I declare that the statements above are true to the best of my information, knowledge and belief.

_____
Date

_____
Name (typed)

_____
Signature

MC 302 (5/88) **PROOF OF MAILING**

Special and Local Forms

Original - Court
1st copy - Applicant
2nd copy - Opposing party
PROBATE OSM CODE: OSF

STATE OF MICHIGAN	AFFIDAVIT AND ORDER	CASE NO.
JUDICIAL DISTRICT JUDICIAL CIRCUIT COUNTY PROBATE	SUSPENSION OF FEES/COSTS	

Court address | Court telephone no.

Plaintiff/Petitioner name, address, and telephone no.

v

Defendant/Respondent name, address, and telephone no.

Plaintiff's/Petitioner's attorney, bar no., address, and telephone no.

Defendant's/Respondent's attorney, bar no., address, and telephone no.

☐ Probate   In the matter of _____

AFFIDAVIT

1. The attached pleading is to be filed with the court by or on behalf of _____ ,
   Name

applicant, who is ☐ plaintiff/petitioner.   ☐ defendant/respondent.

2. The applicant is entitled to and asks the court for suspension of fees and costs in the action for the following reason:

   ☐ a. S/he is currently receiving public assistance: $ _____ per _____ Case No.: _____ .

   ☐ b. S/he is unable to pay those fees and costs because of indigency, based on the following facts:

   INCOME: _____
   Employer name and address

   _____ _____ _____ per ☐ week. ☐ month. ☐ two weeks.
   Length of employment   Average gross pay   Average net pay

   ASSETS: State value of car, home, bank deposits, bonds, stocks, etc.

   OBLIGATIONS: Itemize monthly rent, installment payments, mortgage payments, child support, etc.

   REIMBURSEMENT:
3. (in domestic relations cases only) The applicant is entitled to an order requiring his/her spouse to pay attorney fees.

_____
Affiant signature

Subscribed and sworn to before me on _____ , _____ County, Michigan.
                                        Date

My commission expires: _____   Signature: _____
                        Date   Deputy clerk/Register/Notary public

(SEE REVERSE SIDE FOR ORDER)

CERTIFICATION OF ATTORNEY

1. I have reviewed the affidavit of indigency, and I certify that its contents are true to the best of my information, knowledge, and belief.

2. I will bring to the court's attention the matter of suspended costs and fees and the availability of funds to pay them before any disposition is entered. I will report at that time any changes in the information contained in the affidavit of indigency or any other information regarding the affiant's financial status or alterations of the fee arrangement.

_____
Date

_____
Attorney signature

_____
Attorney name (type or print)   Bar no.

CERTIFICATION BY PERSON OTHER THAN PARTY

1. I have personal knowledge of the facts appearing in the affidavit.

2. The person in whose behalf the petition is filed is unable to sign it because of

☐ minority: _____   ☐ other disability: _____
Date of birth   Nature of disability

Relationship: _____

_____
Date

_____
Affiant signature

_____
Affiant name (type or print)

_____
Address

_____
City, state, zip   Telephone no.

ORDER

IT IS ORDERED:

☐ 1. Fees and costs in this action required by law or court rule are waived/suspended until further order of the court. Before any final disposition or discontinuance is entered, the moving party shall bring the fee and costs suspension to the attention of the judge for final disposition.

2. Requests for waiver/suspension of transcript costs must be made separately by motion.

☐ 3. The applicant's spouse shall pay the fees and costs required by law or court rule.

☐ 4. This application is denied.

_____
Date

_____
Judge   Bar no.

STATE OF MICHIGAN **JUDICIAL DISTRICT** **JUDICIAL CIRCUIT**	**MOTION AND VERIFICATION** **FOR ALTERNATE SERVICE**	**CASE NO.**

Court address _____ Court telephone no.

Plaintiff name(s), address(es), and telephone number(s)		Defendant name(s), address(es), and telephone number(s)
	v	

1. Service of process upon _____ cannot reasonably be made as otherwise provided in MCR 2.105, as shown in the following verification of process server.

2. Defendant's last known home and business addresses are:

Home address	City	State	Zip
Business address	City	State	Zip

    a. I believe the ☐ home / ☐ business address shown above is current.

    b. I do not know defendant's current ☐ home / ☐ business address. I have made the following efforts to ascertain the current address: _____

_____

_____

3. I request the court order service by alternate means.

I declare that the statements above are true to the best of my information, knowledge and belief.

Date _____

Address _____

City, state, zip _____ Telephone no. _____

Attorney signature _____

Attorney name (type or print) _____ Bar no. _____

VERIFICATION OF PROCESS SERVER

1. I have tried to serve process on this defendant as described: State date, place, and what occurred on each occasion

I declare that the statements above are true to the best of my information, knowledge and belief.

Date _____

Signature _____

Process Server (type or print) _____

STATE OF MICHIGAN JUDICIAL DISTRICT JUDICIAL CIRCUIT	ORDER FOR ALTERNATE SERVICE	CASE NO.

Court address	Court telephone no.

Plaintiff name(s), address(es), and telephone no.(s)		Defendant name(s), address(es), and telephone no.(s)
	v	
Plaintiff's attorney, bar no., address, and telephone no.		

THE COURT FINDS:

1. Service of process upon defendant _____

 cannot reasonably be made as provided in MCR 2.105, and service of process may be made in a manner which is reasonably

 calculated to give defendant actual notice of the proceedings and an opportunity to be heard.

IT IS ORDERED:

2. Service of the summons and complaint and a copy of this order may be made by the following method(s):

 a. ☐ First class mail to _____

 b. ☐ Tacking or firmly affixing to the door at _____

 c. ☐ Delivering at _____

 to a member of defendant's household who is of suitable age and discretion to receive process, with instructions to deliver

 it promptly to defendant.

 d. ☐ Other: _____

 _____

3. For each method used, proof of service must be filed promptly with the court.

_____   _____
Date   Judge   Bar no.

MC 304 (8/88) **ORDER FOR ALTERNATE SERVICE**   MCR 2.103, MCR 2.105

PROOF OF SERVICE

I served a copy of the summons and complaint and a copy of the order for alternate service upon

_____ by:

☐ 1. First class mail to _____ , on _____
Date

☐ 2. Tacking or firmly affixing to the door at _____ , on _____
Date

☐ 3. Delivering at _____ , on _____
Date

to a member of defendant's household who is of suitable age and discretion to receive process, with instructions to deliver

it promptly to defendant.

☐ 4. Other: _____ , on _____
Date

_____

Date

_____

Signature

_____

Title

Subscribed and sworn to before me on_____ , _____County, Michigan.
Date

My commission expires: _____ Signature: _____
Date   Deputy court clerk/Notary public

STATE OF MICHIGAN ___ JUDICIAL DISTRICT ___ JUDICIAL CIRCUIT	ORDER FOR SERVICE BY PUBLICATION/POSTING AND NOTICE OF ACTION	CASE NO.

Court address   **Court telephone no.**

Plaintiff name(s) and address(es)		Defendant name(s) and address(es)
	v	
Plaintiff's attorney, bar no., address, and telephone no.		

TO: _____

IT IS ORDERED:

1. You are being sued by plaintiff in this court to _____
_____ . You must file your answer or take other action
permitted by law in this court at the court address above on or before _____ . If you fail to do
<small>Date</small>
so, a default judgment may be entered against you for the relief demanded in the complaint filed in this case.

2. A copy of this order shall be published once each week in _____
               <small>Name of publication</small>
      ☐ three consecutive weeks,
for ☐ _____ , and proof of publication shall be filed in this court.

3. _____ shall post a copy of this order in the courthouse, and
<small>Name</small>
at _____ and
<small>Location</small>
at _____
<small>Location</small>
      ☐ three continuous weeks,
for ☐ _____ , and shall file proof of posting in this court.

4. A copy of this order shall be sent to _____ at the last known address
            <small>Name</small>
          ☐ date of the last publication,
by registered mail, return receipt requested, before the ☐ last week of posting,   and the affidavit of mailing shall be
filed with this court.

_____   _____   Bar no.
Date   Judge

MC 307 (8/88) **ORDER FOR SERVICE BY PUBLICATION/POSTING AND NOTICE OF ACTION**   MCR 2.106

AFFIDAVIT OF PUBLISHING

Name of ☐ publisher ☐ agent of publisher	Attach copy of publication here

Name of newspaper   County where published

This newspaper is a qualified newspaper. The attached copy was published in this newpaper for at least 3 consecutive weeks on these dates:

_____

_____   _____
Date   Affiant signature

Subscribed and sworn to before me on _____ , _____ County, Michigan.
                                      Date

My commission expires: _____ Signature: _____
                      Date   Court clerk/Notary public

AFFIDAVIT OF POSTING

I have posted this order in a conspicuous place in the _____ courthouse and the

following places as ordered by this court: _____

_____

_____

It has been posted for   ☐3 continous weeks   ☐ _____ continuous weeks   as ordered by this court.

_____   _____
Date   Affiant signature

Subscribed and sworn to before me on _____ , _____ County, Michigan.
                                        Date

My commission expires: _____ Signature: _____
                      Date   Court clerk/Notary public

AFFIDAVIT OF MAILING

	Attach mailing receipt and return receipt here

As ordered, on _____ I mailed a copy of the attached summons and
           Date

complaint and this order to _____
                          Name

at _____ .
   Address

The mailing receipt and return receipt are attached at right.

_____   _____
Date   Affiant signature

Subscribed and sworn to before me on _____ , _____ County, Michigan.
                                        Date

My commission expires: _____ Signature: _____
                      Date   Court clerk/Notary public

Approved, SCAO

STATE OF MICHIGAN JUDICIAL CIRCUIT COUNTY	VERIFIED STATEMENT	CASE NO.

1. Mother's last name	First name	Middle name	2. Any other names by which mother is or has been known

3. Date of birth	4. Social security number	5. Driver license number and state

6. Mailing address and residence address (if different)

7. Eye color	8. Hair color	9. Height	10. Weight	11. Race	12. Scars, tattoos, etc.

13. Home telephone no.	14. Work telephone no.	15. Maiden name	16. Occupation

17. Business/Employer's name and address	18. Gross weekly income

19. Has wife applied for or does she receive public assistance? If yes, please specify kind. ☐ Yes ☐ No	20. AFDC and recipient identification numbers

21. Father's last name	First name	Middle name	22. Any other names by which father is or has been known

23. Date of birth	24. Social security number	25. Driver license number and state

26. Mailing address and residence address (if different)

27. Eye color	28. Hair color	29. Height	30. Weight	31. Race	32. Scars, tattoos, etc.

33. Home telephone no.	34. Work telephone no.	35. Occupation

36. Business/Employer's name and address	37. Gross weekly income

38. Has husband applied for or does he receive public assistance? If yes, please specify kind. ☐ Yes ☐ No	39. AFDC and recipient identification numbers

40. a. Name of Minor Child Involved in Case	b. Birth Date	c. Age	d. Soc. Sec. No.	e. Residential Address

41. a. Name of Other Minor Child of Either Party	b. Birth Date	c. Age	d. Soc. Sec. No.	e. Residential Address

42. Health care coverage available for each minor child

a. Name of Minor Child	b. Name of Policy Holder	c. Name of Insurance Co./HMO	d. Policy/Certificate/Contract No.

43. Names and addresses of person(s) other than parties, if any, who may have custody of child(ren) during pendency of this case

• If any of the public assistance information above changes before your judgment is entered, you are required to give the Friend of the Court written notice of the change.

I declare that the statements above are true to the best of my information, knowledge, and belief.

Date _____

Signature _____

FOC 23 (5/93) VERIFIED STATEMENT

MCR 3.206(B)

Request for Certification of Military Status

TO:

Army
Enlisted Records
Fort Benjamin Harrison, IN 46216
Certification fee: $4.50

Navy
World Wide Locator
Bureau of Navy Personnel
PERS-324D
2 Navy Annex
Washington, DC 20370-3240

Marine Corps
Locator Service
USMC-CMC
HQMC-MMSB-10
2008 Elliot Road, Suite 210
Quantico, VA 22134-5030
Certification fee: $3.50 (payable to "U.S. Treasurer")

Air Force
World Wide Locator
AFPC MSIMDL
550C Street West, Suite 50
Randolph Air Force Base, TX 78150-4752

Coast Guard
Commandant, U.S. Coast Guard
Headquarters, Room 4616
2100 2nd St., S.W.
Washington, DC 22059-0001

RE:

Case name _____

Case number _____

Full name of defendant _____

Defendant's social security number _____

Dates of induction and discharge (if known) _____

    I am the plaintiff in the above divorce case, seeking a default judgment of divorce against the defendant. I must know whether or not the defendant is currently in your branch of the U.S. military service, to satisfy the Soldiers' and Sailors' Civil Relief Act of 1940.

    Please respond with a certificate of the defendant's (non)military status, with dates of induction and discharge, if any, as soon as possible. A self-addressed stamped envelope is enclosed for your response, plus any fee for the certification.

Date_____

Signature _____

Name_____

Address _____

_____

Telephone: _____

Approved, SCAO

STATE OF MICHIGAN	DISMISSAL	CASE NO.
JUDICIAL DISTRICT		
JUDICIAL CIRCUIT		
COUNTY PROBATE		

Court address   Court telephone no.

Plaintiff name(s) and address(es)

v

Defendant name(s) and address(es)

Plaintiff's attorney, bar no., address, and telephone no.

Defendant's attorney, bar no., address, and telephone no.

☐ **NOTICE OF DISMISSAL BY PLAINTIFF**

☐ with
☐ without   prejudice as to:

1. Plaintiff/Attorney for plaintiff files this notice of dismissal of this case
   ☐ all defendants.
   ☐ the following defendant(s): _____

2. I certify, under penalty of contempt, that:
   a. This notice is the first dismissal filed by the plaintiff based upon or including the same claim against the defendant.
   b. All costs of filing and service have been paid.
   c. **No answer or motion has been served upon the plaintiff by the defendant** as of the date of this notice.
   d. A copy of this notice has been provided to the appearing defendant/attorney by ☐ mail ☐ personal service.

_____   _____
Date   Plaintiff/Attorney signature

☐ **STIPULATION TO DISMISS**

☐ with
☐ without   prejudice as to:

I stipulate to the dismissal of this case
☐ all parties.
☐ the following parties: _____

_____   _____
Date   Plaintiff/Attorney signature

_____   _____
Date   Defendant/Attorney signature

☐ **ORDER TO DISMISS**

☐ with
☐ without   prejudice. Conditions, if any: _____

IT IS ORDERED this case is dismissed

_____

_____

_____   _____   _____
Date   Judge   Bar no.

MC 09 (6/97) **DISMISSAL**   MCR 2.504

STATE OF MICHIGAN JUDICIAL CIRCUIT COUNTY	INCOME WITHHOLDING ORDER ☐ Court ordered ☐ Consent	CASE NO.

Friend of the Court address

Court telephone no.

Plaintiff's name and address

Regarding: _____
Payer

_____
Social security number

v

Defendant's name and address

Date of order: _____

Judge: _____

1. The court finds that the above payer owes current support, statutory fees, and/or arrearages in the above case, and notice has been given as required by law.

2. Income is defined as: commissions, earnings, salaries, wages, and other income due now or in the future from an employer and successor employers; any payment due now or in the future from a profit-sharing plan, pension plan, insurance contract, annuity, unemployment compensation, supplemental unemployment benefits, and worker's compensation; any amount of money due the payer under a support order as a debt of any other individual, partnership, association, private or public corporation, the United States or any Federal agency, any state or political subdivision of any state, or any other legal entity indebted to the payer.

IT IS ORDERED:

3. The source of income shall withhold payer's income as specified in the attached notice of income withholding and in any subsequent notices.

4. The friend of the court shall be appointed receiver to receive, take possession, cash, and disburse these funds for the purpose of collecting support, statutory fees, and the payment of all arrearages.

5. Any income withheld under this order shall be paid to the friend of the court within 3 days after the date of withholding.

6. If the payer's existing support order is modified by an order of the court, the office of the friend of the court shall send a notice of modification to the source of income by ordinary mail. The amount assigned or withheld shall be changed to conform with the court modification within 7 days after receipt of the notice of modification.

_____
Signature of preparer

_____
Judge

Bar no.

☐ I consent to the terms of this order.

_____
Payer's signature

CERTIFICATE OF MAILING

I certify that on this date I mailed a copy of this order to the parties and sources of income by ordinary mail addressed to the last known addresses.

_____
Date

_____
Signature

FOC 5 (3/96) **INCOME WITHHOLDING ORDER**

MCL 552.601 et seq.; MSA 25.164(1) et seq.

Approved, SCAO

STATE OF MICHIGAN JUDICIAL CIRCUIT COUNTY	AGREEMENT SUSPENDING IMMEDIATE INCOME WITHHOLDING	CASE NO.

Friend of the Court address   Court telephone no.

Plaintiff's name, address, and social security no.

v

Defendant's name, address, and social security no.

NOTE: MCL 552.604(3); MSA 25.164(4)(3) requires that all new and modified support orders after December 31, 1990 include a provision for immediate income withholding and that income withholding take effect immediately unless the parties enter into a written agreement that the income withholding order shall not take effect immediately.

We understand that by law an order of income withholding in a support order shall take effect immediately. However, we agree to the following:

1. The order of income withholding shall not take effect immediately.

2. An alternative payment arrangement shall be made as follows:

3. Both the payer and the recipient of support shall keep the friend of the court informed of the following:
   a. the name and address of his/her current source of income;
   b. any health care coverage that is available to him/her as a benefit of employment or that is maintained by him/her; the name of the insurance company, health care organization, or health maintenance organization; the policy, certificate or contract number; and the name(s) and birth date(s) of the person(s) for whose benefit s/he maintains health care coverage under the policy, certificate, or contract; and
   c. his/her current residence and mailing address.

4. We further understand that proceedings to implement income withholding shall commence if the payer of support falls one month behind in his/her support payments.

5. We recognize that the court may order withholding of income to take effect immediately for cause or at the request of the payer.

_____
Date

_____
Plaintiff's signature

_____
Date

_____
Defendant's signature

FOC 63 (3/93) **AGREEMENT SUSPENDING IMMEDIATE INCOME WITHHOLDING**   MCL 552.604; MSA 25.164(4)

Approved, SCAO

STATE OF MICHIGAN JUDICIAL CIRCUIT COUNTY	ORDER SUSPENDING IMMEDIATE INCOME WITHHOLDING	CASE NO.

Friend of the Court address

Court telephone no.

Plaintiff's name, address, and social security no.

v

Defendant's name, address, and social security no.

1. Date of hearing: _____ Judge: _____

Bar no.

2. **THE COURT FINDS:**

☐ There is good cause for the order of income withholding not to take effect immediately as follows:
  a. It is in the best interest of the child for immediate income withholding not to take effect for the following stated reasons:

  b. Proof of timely payment of previously ordered support has been provided.
  c. Both the payer and the recipient of support will notify the friend of the court in writing of any change in:
    1) the name and address of his/her current source of income;
    2) any health care coverage that is available to him/her as a benefit of employment or that is maintained by him/her, the name of the insurance company, health care organization, or health maintenance organization; the policy, certificate, or contract number; and the names and birth dates of the persons for whose benefit s/he maintains health care coverage under the policy, certificate, or contract; and
    3) his/her current residence and mailing address within 21 days of the change.

☐ The parties have entered into a written agreement that has been reviewed and entered in the record as follows:
  a. The order of income withholding shall not take effect immediately.
  b. An alternative payment arrangement has been agreed upon (attached).
  c. Both the payer and the recipient of support will notify the friend of the court in writing of any change in:
    1) the name and address of his/her current source of income;
    2) any health care coverage that is available to him/her as a benefit of employment or that is maintained by him/her, the name of the insurance company, health care organization, or health maintenance organization; the policy, certificate, or contract number; and the names and birth dates of the persons for whose benefit s/he maintains health care coverage under the policy, certificate, or contract; and
    3) his/her current residence and mailing address within 21 days of the change.

IT IS ORDERED:

3. Income withholding shall not take effect immediately.
4. Income withholding shall take effect if the fixed amount of arrearage is reached, as specified in law.

_____   _____
Date   Judge

FOC 64 (6/94) **ORDER SUSPENDING IMMEDIATE INCOME WITHHOLDING**

MCL 552.511; MSA 25.176(11),
MCL 552.604; MSA 25.164(4) .
MCL 552.607; MSA 25.164(7)

Penobscot Bldg. 645 Griswold Ave. Detroit, MI 48226   *313-224-5372*

PLAINTIFF'S NAME		DEFENDANT'S NAME
	V.	

I certify the attached Order or Judgment as presented for entry to be in full conformity with the requirements set forth by statute, INCLUDING A PROVISION FOR IMMEDIATE INCOME WITHHOLDING (WHICH SHALL BE IMPLEMENTED BY THE FRIEND OF THE COURT), THE PAYER'S SOCIAL SECURITY NUMBER AND THE NAME AND ADDRESS OF HIS/HER SOURCE OF INCOME IF KNOWN , UNLESS OTHERWISE ORDERED BY THE COURT, and with Michigan Court Rules 3.201 and following, and if applicable, includes all provisions of the Friend of the Court recommendation or is in conformity with the decision of

_____ rendered on the _____ day of

_____ , 19 _____ .

_____

Date

_____

Attorney / Bar No.

Instructions : Please sign and present this Certificate to the Court Clerk when the Order or Judgment is presented for entry. If an ex parte interim order is being presented to the Judge, please complete the "Certificate on Behalf of Plaintiff regarding Ex Parte Interim Support Order" and follow Local Court Rule 3.206.